IN DANGER

*How to Become a Safe Driver
and Avoid Getting Hit*

Dimitry Salchev

ISBN: 979-8-9891155-0-1 (Paperback)
       979-8-9891155-1-8 (eBook)

First Edition

Contents

Introduction

This is a guide book that will take you through every detail of my driving experiences. Its purpose is to share with you my knowledge in order to keep you safe on the road. With over 15,000 passengers served as a rideshare driver and more than 5,000 deliveries completed under my name, I have a unique experience that you will find quite useful. Over the past five years, I have dedicated myself to this profession. As I write this, I continue to be an active rideshare driver, and the number of passengers I serve continues to grow. Ensuring the safety of my passengers is my utmost priority, and I strive to provide a smooth and comfortable ride without any frustrations or the possibility of car crashes. I have driving experience with a diverse range of passengers, from mothers with their infants to seniors with walkers. Furthermore, my driving portfolio offers valuable tips and insights on how to identify and prevent encounters with unsafe drivers, ultimately helping you avoid car accidents and, most importantly, ensuring your safe return home to your family. To me, driving is not just a skill but a science, and through this book I will prove it to you. I want you to become a safe driver, just like me. My ultimate goal is to keep you safe on the road for the sake of all drivers, motorcyclists, bicyclers, and pedestrians.

This book is a little different from others of its sort. You might ask, "Why?" What sets this book apart from others is its unique approach. In addition to written content, each chapter will provide you with exclusive access to short videos on my YouTube channel, allowing you to witness real-life situations on the road that I will reference throughout the book. You can also go to my YouTube channel: https://www.youtube.com/@Dsalchev/videos and have the inventory of the videos ready as I will be referencing them in the chapters in this guide book. The purpose of these videos is to help you learn and understand the behaviors of other drivers and unique situations while you are behind the wheel. It is not just about writing sentences or paragraphs for the sake of the book, I am trying to help you become a safe driver, the one who goes home safe with less frustration on the road. Are you ready? Let's get started.

CHAPTER 1

Getting a Driver's License

LEARN TO BE COMFORTABLE IN YOUR VEHICLE SO YOU CAN SHINE AS A GOOD DRIVER, JUST AS YOUR CAR SHINES

First things first, we all need a driver's license in order to operate a vehicle legally and safely. I know, this sentence sounds more like blah-blah-blah. However, this is where we all have started and the stories I am about to share with you will indicate what I have done before I even became a safe driver. I will take you back to my beginnings on the road to show you what type of driver I was. So, let's delve into my journey and explore the lessons I have learned along the way.

Back in 2009, while I was still living in my country of birth, Bulgaria, I decided to apply for a driver's license. I had to operate a vehicle with a manual transmission or what they call a "gearbox", because at the time, that was the only kind of car available to learn how to drive. Learning to operate a vehicle with manual transmission can indeed be challenging. It requires simultaneous coordination of the clutch pedal and gear shift. If you fail to synchronize these actions correctly, the car will stall unexpectedly, which can be embarrassing and potentially put you in a risky situation on the road. It took me some time to get used to this technique. I recall the very first time I ever drove a vehicle. It was a nightmare. I was in a student's car with my instructor, a man with piercing eyes whom I deeply feared. At the time, I pressed the gas pedal when I was supposed to hit the brake, nearly causing a disaster. The driving instructor yelled at me as if he was about wallop my ass (excuse my French). His piercing eyes made him look like a villain from a scary movie. I couldn't comprehend why the instructor screamed at me that much, considering I had never driven before. However, after a month, I passed the writing and driving exam and obtained my driver's license. Here is my point: **I got my driver's license, but I didn't feel comfortable behind the wheel.**

A year later, on a particular day at work, the foreman of the company that I worked for, had told me to park the company car inside the property where we worked. It didn't strike me as a big deal, so I was excited about the opportunity, even though

I had never done it before. Actually, to be honest with you, I was extremely nervous, but that didn't discourage me. Without realizing the consequences, I jumped in the car and drove into a gate, which was being made from expensive stones, and as soon as I passed through it, I heard an unpleasant screeching noise coming from the right side of the vehicle. Then, my inner voice whispered, "*Damn! I messed up the car!*" The next moment, I jumped out of the vehicle to survey the damages. The right side was scratched badly. Both doors and the fender were visibly damaged, indicating the need for extensive bodywork on the car. So, why am I sharing this with you? The purpose of my story is to alert you to not make the same mistake as I did. I made this mistake because I hadn't felt comfortable operating the car. That said, it is important to learn to be calm and patient behind the wheel, especially if you have only just received your license without much practice.

Getting a Driver's License in the USA

I was in Michigan when I decided to get a driver's license for the first time in the U.S. The instructor was a nice guy. We talked casually about my country throughout the driving exam. At that time, I was operating a van which was perfectly well maintained. The driving exam went fine, except that I almost got into a car accident. How did that happen? Well, the traffic light was green for the cars traveling straight, but red for those in my lane waiting to turn left. Suddenly, I decided that I could quickly make the left turn and cut in front of the cars coming from the opposite direction. I then immediately realized that this was a terrible mistake and promptly hit the brakes, understanding the risk of a potential car accident. As I hit the brakes, I saw how this almost gave the instructor a heart attack. I said to myself, *"There is no way I can pass this driving exam."* To my surprise, I passed. The next week, they mailed my driver's license and I was ready to go.

Here's my point. Even though I had the DL, I didn't feel comfortable behind the wheel. We all have to go through the process of getting to the point where we feel absolutely comfortable behind the steering wheel. The question here is: **how you can learn to be comfortable while operating your vehicle?** Here is the answer: practice driving in rural areas where the traffic is much less or none. To my knowledge, that is the most efficient way to learn to be comfortable behind the wheel, because no one else is around you, which allows you to concentrate on the road and what you are doing. Do it until you get to the point where you can start having fun while you operate your vehicle. Get a buddy with you or ride along with someone with more experience than you, just to make you feel more comfortable. At first, start with a couple of minutes. Then, do it more often. Drive two or three times a week to a countryside area where cars are barely visible. Important note: **I'm not telling you to go on a road trip, drinking beers or smoking blunts while you operate your vehicle.** Just free your mind and go for a ride. Make yourself comfortable. Listen to your favorite song on the radio. Make your automobile your best buddy. What do I mean by that? Enjoy the ride and have fun, but don't get too cocky. That is something I will talk about later.

Getting a License in Illinois

Important note: since I have been living and driving in Chicago at this point in my life, I will talk about driving mostly in the Windy City, but my methods could be applied anywhere. Something else I need to emphasize here: I will be repeating subjects and topics as well as phrases in this book to help you understand the importance of each subject. So, are you ready? Let's get started.

In 2014, my job assignments were finished, and I had to relocate from Michigan to Illinois. Moving to a new State meant changing my driver's license. I got my Illinois driving license in the beginning of 2015. I passed the writing test easily because I studied for that exam for two weeks straight. The driving test was done in Deerfield, IL, considered one of the best neighborhoods in the State. The roads were clean, without any potholes. The streets were mostly empty and easy to get around on. Nothing really to worry about.

At that time, I drove a Geo Prizm, which was an old car but it ran well. When the instructor jumped into my car, I became a little nervous because I didn't know where we would go and how long I would be driving. But that didn't bother me too much because at this point, I was already comfortable behind the wheel. After twenty minutes of driving, I passed the test without any issues. Even the instructor complimented on my driving because I had done an immaculate job. It was so easy, as if had done it a million times already. Here is my point: even though I had the license without any problems, I didn't feel experienced enough, knowing that I still had much more to learn.

Learn to Be Comfortable Behind the Steering Wheel

Driving comes easier after you learn to be comfortable behind the steering wheel. To do this, you need to make sure that your seat meets your desired level of comfort. Adjust the seat's recliner to a position that ensures you feel comfy while operating your vehicle. Also, make sure that your toes can fully reach the brake and gas pedals for optimal control.

Another crucial aspect of ensuring comfort while you are behind the wheel is to properly adjust your mirrors to enhance visibility. Both the side mirrors and the rearview mirror should be set up correctly. The side mirrors should be positioned in a way that allows you to see the rear side of your vehicle, but only a small portion of it. This is crucial, especially when changing lanes, as it helps you gauge the distance between your vehicle and others. I know, most of you might say, "Blah-blah-blah." But it's important to have a clear understanding of how to adjust your side mirrors because the outcome of doing so correctly is essential. That said, an important thought crosses my mind: **the more comfortable you feel behind the wheel, the better driver you will become.**

What Actually Is a Safe Driver?

First and foremost, before becoming a safe driver, we need to understand what it truly means. A safe driver is not just someone who complies with the rules of the road or knows how to drive properly and smoothly. No! A safe driver is someone who drives defensively, is always aware of their surroundings, and knows how to take actions to avoid car accidents. Also, safe drivers recognize what types of drivers are around them and have the ability to keep a proper distance from them. It is important to understand that a safe driver is a synonym for a patient driver. Let me emphasize something important: **there is no such thing as being a safe driver while exhibiting impatience on the road.** Furthermore, safe drivers don't allow their frustrations to affect their driving, as they know that such impulses are pointless and can only escalate into road rage, which is something everyone should strive to avoid. To become a safe driver, you need to have abilities that distinguish you as an exceptional driver. Ergo, it is an important step to developing your skill set. With that being said, you might be wondering: what is this guy talking about? Bear with me during the next chapter.

CHAPTER 2

Develop Your Skill Set

THE MORE SELF-AWARE YOU ARE, THE SAFER DRIVER YOU WILL BE

As I mentioned earlier, developing your skill set is the technique that sets you apart as a distinguished driver. The one who knows what to do in unpleasant and dangerous situations. The word "aware" is crucial here. It is important to know that you have to be aware of what is going on around you. The best drivers are those who are aware of what is happening around them because they can respond when other drivers make careless or dangerous maneuvers. Well, according to insurance companies, there is a perspective that the best drivers are these drivers who barely drive anywhere. But we will cover this subject later on.

We all have experienced situations where other drivers cut us off or make bizarre maneuvers in front of our eyes, or drivers who think themselves master champions, recklessly overtaking others at dangerously high speeds. Also, it is important to keep an eye out for slower moving vehicles, bicycles, and pedestrians. In this chapter, I will share with you my knowledge on how to effectively navigate and handle these aspects that surround us while driving.

Checking Your Mirrors

First and foremost, you have to check your mirrors before you even start driving your vehicle. This is one of the most important aspects while you are operating your car. Once you develop this habit, I guarantee that you will feel more comfortable and aware of what others do around you. Let's start with the side mirrors. The side mirrors are built to keep you aware of what is happening on both sides of your car. Before you think about changing lanes or performing any other maneuvers, always check your side mirrors. Side mirrors are designed to keep you aware of what is happening in your blind spots. This is a basic information that every driver should know, but many disregard it. A lot of drivers do not pay enough attention on the side mirrors and that is why they get surprised at the last minute. The side mirrors tell you if subjects such as bicycles are approaching. That is very important because a cyclist may assume that you are watching them. In fact, many cyclists in Chicago rely on the drivers to watch for them, but in most cases, drivers don't have a clue if a cyclist is approaching until it is too late. Don't get me wrong:

I'm not telling you to stare at the side mirrors, you have to learn how to glance at them and quickly look back in front of you. Remember: **watch your side mirrors before it is too late.**

Here is a story of mine that you may find interesting. One day, my car was parked on the street, as I waited to pick up a passenger. At the moment when the passenger hopped in my car, I was ready to go. But before I moved, I looked at my side mirrors to ensure it was safe to proceed. Indeed, on my left side, I saw a white car coming out from a side street that was a few feet away. Suddenly, after it passed me, the car made a hard right turn and drove into the driveway of McDonald's, just a couple of feet ahead of me. It all happened so quickly, within a matter of seconds. Now, if I hadn't looked at my side mirror and if I had decided just to proceed…then, BOOM! I would have hit the car that came from behind in the blink of an eye. This is just a simple example of why it is so important to check your mirrors.

Don't Trust the Blind Spot Sensors

Even though newer cars have sensors that will alert for approaching vehicles in your blinds spots, it remains essential to cultivate the habit of consistently checking your mirrors. You may ask yourself why. Because blind spot sensors don't always work as they should. This is very important. Allow me to share with you a story from my driving portfolio that would illustrate my point. It takes us back to 2019 when my car was in the shop due to an unfortunate accident where a reckless driver had hit me. To continue working as a rideshare driver, I had to rent a car. The rideshare company provided me with a new car equipped with blind spot sensors, which presented a great opportunity for me to experience how these sensors worked. I must say, whoever invented these sensors must not have been a very knowledgeable driver. You may ask yourself why. The blind spot sensors are designed to identify objects that are already within your danger zone. They indicate if a car is two to four feet behind your rear bumper, which is already quite late for you to react. Just think about it. On empty highways, cars can be speeding at 90 to 110 miles per hour. If you are not checking your side mirrors, and rely solely on blind spot sensors, it could already be too late. Hear me out. I am not saying that those sensors won't protect you from dangerous situations; all I am saying is that the sensors do not always provide an accurate idea where the other objects are near you. With this rental car, I also noticed that the sensors weren't always indicating if a car was nearby. Now, I cannot tell you if these sensors weren't functioning correctly due to some mechanical problems, and the car needed additional maintenance. All I am saying is this: the side mirror sensors are not always a safe method of indicating the approach of other vehicles.

Remember: **this is my driving experience and I reveal this information to keep you safe on the roads.**

Watch Out for Other Drivers Because They Won't Watch Out for You

So what do I mean by that? Let me give you a specific situation to better illustrate what I am talking about. In the summer of 2022, I drove a passenger through the West Side of Chicago. The GPS directed me to take Lake Street, which has an elevated train track running above it and columns supporting the tracks. There are additional lanes on each side of the street, divided by these columns. As I was driving on Lake Street, I noticed a white vehicle on my right side, traveling in the extra lane divided by those columns. The white vehicle was driving at over 35 miles per hour when, all of a sudden, it decided to make a left turn right in front of me. I had to hit the brakes and tilt my car to the left side to avoid colliding with the white vehicle. If I hadn't performed this maneuver, we would have been involved in a brutal T-bone accident. So, how did I manage to avoid this unpleasant situation? I was able to prevent it because I had been keeping an eye on the white car on my right side and was prepared for any sudden actions. However, I wasn't intently watching the car, but rather just being aware of it. The guy operating that car mistakenly believed that there was a traffic light ahead, but in reality, the glare from the sun dazzled and completely confused him. There was no traffic light or any stop signs or anything like that. I had to wait and let the white car go first because it had blocked the street. Unexpectedly, just as the white car that nearly collided with me passed by, another vehicle abruptly cut me off from the right side. It was ridiculous. This explains why so many drivers in Chicago drive with the attitude: "I need to be before you. So, screw you!" Please, do yourself a favor. Go on my YouTube channel and look at the video titled "That was close!" (https://youtu.be/9TN7JGelAJ4). The video takes only twenty seconds, but it is long enough to reveal the situation I am talking about above. This is why it is so important to yield for other drivers and be aware of who is around you.

Check Your Rearview Mirror

It is important to constantly check your rearview mirror. Again, don't stare at it, just throw a quick glimpse to have an idea of what the drivers behind you are doing. Please, allow yourself a second to check your rearview mirror and then immediately switch your focus back to the road in front of you.

Important note: make sure that the rearview mirror has been adjusted properly so you won't have issues looking at it.

Speaking of rearview mirrors, another point comes to mind. It is true that some vehicles, like big commercial trucks or specific vans, may not have rearview mirrors. However, these vehicles often have larger and additional side mirrors to provide a better view of the road.

On the highways with more than two lanes in each direction, checking the rearview mirror is crucial. You might ask yourself why? Hear me out. Often cocky drivers will rush on the highways at dangerously fast speeds. They switch lanes in order to go faster as they think they are something extraordinary. These drivers may not wait or may not pay attention to your lane-switching signal, and that can be fatal.

Please, go to my YouTube channel and look at a video called "Hit and run! 2022" (https://youtu.be/zVu3zIDBo9w). In the video, I drove on Kennedy I-90 westbound from downtown Chicago to O'Hare Airport. Back then, I had two passengers with me. The traffic on the highway was mild, the cars moved with around 20 mph. At that time, my vehicle was in the farthest right lane on the highway. As I was watching the road in front of me, which every driver would normally do, then I heard BOOM! My car shook, but it didn't spin. The next moment, I realized that an SUV hit me from the rear. It then cut me off and took the ramp on my right side. Thankfully, my passengers weren't injured, and they didn't require medical assistance, but I still had to chase the vehicle because it hit me and fled the scene. Unfortunately, I couldn't pursue it further because I had passengers with me, so I made sure to document the license plate number and called 911. Here is my point: if I had been checking my rearview mirror, I might have avoided this unpleasant car crash. That said, I need you to understand that I am not claiming to be the best driver in the world. I am sharing this story to encourage you to beware of similar situations, and most importantly, avoid getting hit by consistently checking your rearview mirror.

Check Your Rear Mirror for Impatient Drivers

There are different types of drivers. Here, I will talk about the so-called "Impatient drivers." The next possible question should be: who is the impatient driver? Impatient drivers are those drivers that won't wait for you and will do everything possible to be ahead of you, even if that can cost them getting into a car accident. This is why you have to learn to be aware of such drivers because they can put you into an unpleasant situation. Oftentimes, an impatient driver will be behind you and will tailgate you and honk at you for no apparent reason. That behavior can easily escalate into a road rage or even a car accident. For this reason, it is important to be vigilant and watch for these types of drivers. You might ask how? Check constantly your rearview mirror. Study their behavior and what they do behind your back. This is why being self-aware of what is happening around you is so crucial. This reminds me to emphasize: **you don't want to have impatient driver behind you as they may push your buttons and provoke you**.

Here is how I usually deal with impatient drivers who tailgate me. Play the video called "Tailgating me" (https://youtu.be/8HyTcQIAJgE). The video demonstrates how I was driving on a side street. There was someone tailgating me and pushing me from behind. So, I quickly checked the rearview mirror and safely pulled over to the side to let the impatient driver pass in front of me. Just a moment after the impatient driver went past me, I checked the rearview mirror again and noticed there was no one else behind, so I promptly pulled back into traffic. As you can see, the impatient driver was going too fast and nearly caused a car accident due to their unruly behavior. Here is my point: your mission is to prevent car accidents and ensure the safety of yourself and your passengers. Another point needs to be stated: if you can't pull over, be careful when dealing with an impatient driver who is driving behind you, as they may drive you nuts.

Stay Focused While You are on the Road

I remember once I drove a passenger in downtown Chicago. It was early morning, and the streets were busy, which was quite typical for the city. While I was driving, I actually found myself thinking about a Ukrainian girl whom I have recently connected with on the dating app "Tinder." This girl was absolutely gorgeous and incredibly smart. I mean, she spoke five different languages, not to mention that she was also a neurologist. Anyway, as I was driving, my passenger politely said, "It's okay! You can drop me off here, at this corner!" Baffled, I glimpsed at the GPS and realized that I was supposed to make a left, instead of going straight as I had done. The next moment I pulled to the corner as the passenger had requested, and started apologizing for my mistake. The passenger just quietly left the car, but it was plain to me that I should have paid more attention to the road and less about some gorgeous girl that I had met on Tinder. I came to the horrifying conclusion that I have become a distracted driver without even realizing it at the time. That said, there is an important lesson here: **safe drivers aren't just physically behind the wheel, but they are mentally focused and alert to what is happening around them.**

This story wasn't the only time when I caught myself daydreaming while driving, but I make a conscious effort to avoid such distractions and minimize them as much as possible. I take driving seriously because I drive people and people drive around me. Distracting myself by thinking about something else while driving is unacceptable.

Conclusion: we should refrain from pondering over matters that clearly bother us while we are on the road. Whether it concerns credit card debt, depression, issues with our significant other or family, feelings of anxiety, or in my case thinking about hot chicks. Each of these types of distractions can impact our ability to focus and make us more susceptible to becoming distracted drivers, posing a danger on the road.

Keep It Safe Altogether

Keep it safe altogether. What do I mean by that? Hear me out: you must constantly check your side mirrors, and don't forget about the rearview mirror. This is a habit that you need to cultivate through consistent practice. Check your left and right mirrors every 3-4 seconds, then briefly observe what is happening in front of you. After that, glance at your rearview mirror. As you complete this cycle try to repeat it consistently. If you don't feel comfortable, start by checking only your side mirrors. Then, you can check the rearview mirror. Do it until you build this habit. Let me tell you something: **if you consistently check your mirrors, I guarantee you will come to realize what is happening around you**. You will became aware of what others do, which is why it is crucial to feel at ease while operating your vehicle. Give yourself room to build this driving pattern and you will became a safe and good driver. It is essential to understand that many people are driving on autopilot. They drive from point A to point B without realizing how they got there because their minds are preoccupied with problems at work, or issues with their families, additional anxiety, financial stress, mental breakdowns and so on. We are all have been there. People who are preoccupied or deeply concerned about matters that significantly impact their lives may exhibit behaviors such as cutting you off, disregarding stop signs, or engaging in other actions that may be unsafe or inconsiderate. Additionally, they may not pay attention on the road as they should. This is why you have to learn to be careful for your own safety. Let me ask you this: what is the most important point of driving your vehicle? The answer is simple: to return safely to your family. Nobody wants to be involved in a car accident. For this reason, you must learn how to protect yourself from other drivers. And this is what exactly I will cover in the next chapter. Are you ready? Let's jump in.

CHAPTER 3

Different Types of Drivers

DRIVING ISN'T ABOUT GOING SOMEWHERE FIRST. IT IS ABOUT GETTING BACK HOME SAFELY!

Now you know the importance of being comfortable behind the wheel by checking your mirrors persistently. The next questions is: what do you need to look for? Or what do you need to be aware of? One of the most significant and perilous elements on the road is the other drivers. Always keep in mind that you must watch out for them because they won't look out for you. That being noted, let's break down the different types of drivers on the road. In this chapter, we will explore and discuss the various categories of drivers.

1. Impatient Drivers

Yes, I mentioned those drivers the previous chapter, but it is essential to reiterate their behavior on the streets. First thing first, the question comes across: what does an impatient driver do? Once again, impatient drivers don't pay attention to you. They will do anything possible to get ahead of you. They are so obsessed with the idea of getting in front of you that they are willing to take any risk in order to do so. An impatient driver will honk at you pretty much anywhere for a reason or no reason at all, especially if they are behind you on the side streets. Again, avoiding these types of drivers is fundamental because they can put you in an unpleasant situation.

When you are stuck in heavy traffic on the highways, the impatient driver is most likely to keep switching lanes in an attempt to move faster. In those scenarios, the chances of an impatient driver cutting you off are high. For that reason, you must watch out for these drivers. Reading this, you may say in response, "Yes, but I am not a mind-reader!" Here's the great part: I am not a mind-reader either. Studying and recognizing the impatient driver or any other type of driver isn't about mind reading. It has nothing to do with it.

To help you become self-aware, I decided to make it more interesting, and uploaded a video on my YouTube channel called "Impatient driver 2" (https://youtu.be/36IbHCzEb_M). In this video, I smoothly switched lanes while checking the driver on my right side. The next second, an SUV decided to cut me off in order to move faster. Prepared for this kind of abrupt maneuver, I reacted quickly without getting into a car accident. I hit the brakes and allowed the impatient driver to go in front of me. Let me tell you something: **if I hadn't stopped, the SUV would have hit me**. In fact, I can say with certainty that the SUV driver was completely unaware of my vehicle. This is why you need to be careful and watch out for other drivers, as they may not be watching out for you. Remember: **avoid staring at other drivers, but instead, take quick glances at them and always keep in mind that they may cut you off.**

There is another video that displays the behavior of impatient drivers. Go to my YouTube channel and watch a 40 second video called "An impatient driver" (https://youtu.be/KSUT4ailv_I). In this video, you can see how I patiently waited for a limo driver to do a parallel parking. Since there was only one lane in each direction, I made the decision to wait for the limo to finish parking, which took no more than 5 to 6 seconds. Initially, everything was going fine, but there was an impatient driver behind me who started honking anxiously. In that situation, I couldn't do anything but wait for the limo driver to complete the parking. After that, as I drove ahead, I noticed that the impatient driver behind me was trying to overtake me. I thought to myself, "*Why is this person rushing so much?*" In the next few seconds, the impatient driver drove past me on my left side and barely made it through the traffic light as it turned yellow. I doubt if that impatient driver would have stopped even for a red light. As you can tell, the impatient driver had no intention of stopping and put themselves and others around them in serious danger. Fortunately, nothing happened at that moment, but that doesn't mean the impatient driver should have done it in the first place. This is why it is so important to avoid these types of drivers as the utmost priority for us is to return home safely to our families.

To help you better understand what impatient drivers are really like, I have uploaded a video titled "This is crazy!" (https://youtu.be/OTNtyxqzVqo). As you can see, I was driving on a busy street when suddenly the driver of a white minivan, coming from a side street on my right, decided to disregard my right of way and performed a kamikaze-like maneuver by making a left turn in front of me, leaving me with no choice but to come to a full stop in order to avoid a car wreck. This video epitomizes what an impatient driver and their behavior on the street are like. They won't wait for you and will attempt to get in front of you, even though that could put everyone else in danger. Now, as I am watching the video, it crosses my mind that the white minivan driver might have assumed that I had a stop sign, which, as it clearly shows, wasn't the case. However, the purpose of this material is to raise awareness about impatient drivers, similar to the one featured in the video.

Also, you should be careful if you have to drive in early mornings, especially around 4:00 and 5:00 a.m. At that time, impatient drivers would drive as fast as possible because the highways or the streets are empty. When I used to drive in those morning hours, I was often baffled. Once, an impatient driver cut me off from the right side just as the shoulder was bottlenecking. I had no choice but to hit the brakes and allow the impatient driver to go ahead of me. Let me make something clear: we all want to get where we are going as quickly as possible. I get that. Safe drivers also need to drive fast at times. But they still manage to do it in a safe way, without causing risky situations on the streets. As for impatient drivers, they will do anything possible, putting lives in danger, in order to reach their destinations as soon as they can. This reminds me to ask the question—**is it really worth it for these drivers to risk their lives and others' lives to get to their destination a few minutes earlier?**

We all know that on a daily basis, there are many impatient drivers. They will sneak in and try anything possible to be in front of us. For this reason, it is our responsibility to keep distance from them because it can get ugly.

2. Reckless Drivers

Reckless drivers are all types of drivers who drive under influence of alcohol and drugs. Be careful of them as they can put you into a dangerous situation. In Chicago, you can mostly spot them on Friday and Saturday night. I say Chicago, but I am sure this applies in other cities as well. Also, you can see many reckless drivers on the holidays, for example the 4th of July. During the summertime, I witness those drivers zooming on the highways and darting between lanes in a wild manner. It is mostly young people who engage in this behavior, either heading to big parties or simply speeding without any particular reason. Reckless drivers won't watch out for you, because they don't care about you. Moreover, they would cut you off and speed as fast as they could possibly go. Stay away from them. You don't need to be around them.

I have come across another category of reckless drivers who drive excessively slowly, causing frustration as they struggle to maintain their vehicle within a single lane. In many instances, these drivers have consumed alcohol and are attempting to adhere to the speed limit while making their way home. Once again, stay away from those drivers. Be aware of their behavior as getting involved with them can potentially lead to a dangerous situation. I know, I sound like an old-timer rideshare driver who reiterates clichés here and there, but I think this information can save your life.

3. Cocky Drivers

Cocky drivers are similar to "Reckless drivers." You might ask yourself, "What is the difference?" Cocky drivers tend to underestimate the seriousness of driving and are inclined to perform risky maneuvers for no apparent reason. They intentionally accelerate their cars as they perceive themselves as Lewis Hamilton. A cocky driver will rush down the highway as if they are in a race. In most cases, you can encounter these drivers on the weekends in the summertime. Often, they are riding along with their buddies. Their philosophy is simple—to prove you how good they are and how fast they can drive. Cocky drivers are delusional, taking driving for granted and perceiving themselves as someone extraordinary on the road, thinking they are better than everyone around them. Let me tell you something—I don't see these *professional* drivers when it snows. Conclusion: watch out for them and most importantly stay away from them.

4. Confused Drivers

We can't go any further without mentioning these types of drivers. I think we all agree that a confused driver is dangerous for others. The good thing about confused drivers is that they are not hard to recognize. In downtown Chicago, I see many confused drivers, especially during the summertime. They simply drive too slowly because they are persistently looking at their GPS, trying to decide on which direction should go. This reminds me to emphasize: **a confused driver can make an abrupt maneuver that can be fatal for you.** Stay away from them. Try to avoid getting too close to them, as they have a tendency to easily frustrate or anger you with their foolish actions.

Let me share a story with you. The first year I came to Chicago, I was a disaster when it comes to driving. I was taking wrong ways, making weird decisions, and yada-yada. My first year as a rideshare driver was horrible too. I had to learn how to drive in downtown Chicago on my own, without any assistance or advice. It was a tough assignment, but I didn't quit. I was determined not to be the kind of driver who would frustrate others. Whenever I felt confused or uncertain about which street to take, I would pull over safely and study the GPS. In that case, I wasn't a problem for other drivers, and to be honest with you, it worked like a charm. To me, learning how to drive in downtown was an ongoing process, but I managed it in a profound and safe way. At the moment I am writing this, I can boldly confess that driving in downtown is as simple as taking pictures with my smartphone. Joking aside, the point

I am trying to make here is that you must always keep an eye out for confused drivers.

5. Distracted Drivers

Nowadays, many drivers frequently use their phones while operating their vehicles. It is essential to emphasize that using a phone while driving is dangerous. A driver who engages with their phone becomes distracted and fails to give proper attention to the road. This issue has been a significant problem for years. Hear me out: I am not talking about the people who are connected to their phones via Bluetooth or other hands-free devices. I am talking about these drivers who play with their smartphones, look at their social media, text, etc. You need to understand: **it takes only a second for a car accident to occur.** With that being said, it boils down to this— every time a driver takes their eyes off the road, they are taking a huge risk of getting involved in a car accident. Do me a favor, next time you are stuck in traffic on the highway, glimpse at the drivers next to you. Make a quick note of their behavior behind the wheel. You will be surprised of how many people are using their phones while driving in heavy traffic, especially drivers in their early twenties. I have witnessed hundreds, if not thousands of drivers, swiping through social media while driving on jammed highways. Those drivers are often oblivious to their surroundings as they choose to check their social media, text, and engage in other distractions. It is paramount to remember that an unaware driver is a dangerous driver. This is why self-awareness is a crucial aspect when it comes to driving. With these thoughts in mind, there is something else that needs to be addressed—GPS. According to *utires.com*, studies show that 93% percent of people being asked responded that they would likely use a GPS device while driving. Of which, 83% of respondents said they would get lost without their GPS.

Another fact you need to keep in mind, as we talk about distracted drivers, is that I have often seen some of these drivers operating their vehicles with folded-in side mirrors. I can't help but wonder how these drivers manage to drive their vehicles like that. This takes me to another important point: if you ever encounter a driver with folded-in side mirrors next to you, I would suggest keeping a safe distance from them. Who knows what they are looking at while operating their vehicles?

6. Unaware Drivers

Unaware drivers usually take driving for granted. They don't pay attention on the roads and often cannot recall how they get from point A to point B. These drivers don't drive much and have no interest in driving; they simply reach their destination with indifference. To make it more captivating, I uploaded a video called "Another crazy driver 3" that clearly demonstrates the bizarre behavior of an unaware driver (https://youtu.be/WXDUgrpQD-Q). As I was driving early in the morning, out of the blue, a vehicle started backing up without having any visibility. Surprised by this unaware driver, I had to hit the brakes and veer off my vehicle to avoid a potential car accident. Now, I cannot really explain why the driver decided to do a kamikaze-like maneuver by reversing their vehicle on a busy street early in the morning without any clear visibility, but I can firmly declare that this unware driver was very lucky at that time. This reminds me to emphasize: **unware drivers are extremely dangerous and we should keep an eye on them.** What I have experienced lately is that the number of unaware drivers has increased significantly, and that concerns me on a large scale. For this reason, I suggest you to study their behavior as they may put your life in danger.

7. Unexperienced Drivers

Unexperienced drivers can be very dangerous on the streets. They may drive too slowly or do unpredictable maneuvers like switching lanes improperly, abruptly stopping, etc. Some of them may have bumper stickers saying "Student Driver," but not all of them. These types of drivers can get on your nerves if you are around them. Thus, it is important to keep a safe distance from them.

Another important aspect to be aware of is that a cocky driver could also be an inexperienced driver. They might intentionally speed excessively to demonstrate their driving skills. Once again, I emphasize the need to maintain a safe distance from them, as they can put you in a risky situation.

8. Senior Drivers

Let me make myself clear; I don't hold any grudges or have anything against seniors. I don't dislike them and never engage in confrontations with them. When I am saying be aware of senior drivers I don't mean *every* single one of them is a hazard—I'm just saying that *some* of them could be dangerous. You may ask yourself, "Why this guy is bringing all this up?" I am sharing this because I have seen many situations in which seniors get involved in car accidents or even hitting cyclists. Here is one of them. In the summer of 2019, I was driving a passenger on Fullerton Street by Lake Shore Drive. A blue Toyota was waiting to make a left turn on N. Stockton Dr. Suddenly, the Toyota driver decided to switch the lanes and merged onto the right side where other vehicles were driving straight ahead. The Toyota's driver failed to see properly and hit an Uber driver who, at that time, happened to be driving forward. It was a brutal car accident that occurred in front of my eyes. I saw the Toyota driver was a senior who apparently had made a tremendous mistake.

Senior drivers usually drive less often than others. They can have slower reaction times and take longer to respond to dangerous situations than they should. Again, don't get me wrong; I am not trying to insult anyone by saying that. This information is based on my observation and my experience behind the wheel.

Ironically, the best driver I know is actually a senior. This is my old man. Yes, indeed. My father is the best driver I ever met. He is from the baby boomer generation, and in his time things were different compared to the digital era. Dad is a self-taught person (I wonder from where I got this skill). In his time, Dad had to learn how to operate a vehicle on his own. Surely, he had to take a driving test to obtain a driver's license, but he had taught himself how to operate a vehicle. He was twenty-five when he started participating in race tournaments back in my country of birth. In the 90s, my father became a time-attack racing driver who competed actively for a few years and won several medals. Unfortunately, over the years Dad struggled to find a good sponsor and he eventually decided to quit his racing career as the expenses would have to be covered out of his pocket. Then, my old man decided to become a cab driver and he has been driving ever since. I am talking about over 30 years of cab driving experience on the streets of Plovdiv, Bulgaria. Let me tell you something; if there is someone who should write a book about driving that surely is my old man.

I remember in my high school years, I used to ride along with my father. On rare occasions, he would pick me up from school, and we would drive around the city. At that time, I was watching him operate his vehicle. The way he drove a stick-shift made it seem like he had invented the automobile himself. Unfortunately, Dad had never really taught me how to drive and as the years went by, we didn't get along, and I ended up teaching myself how to safely operate a vehicle. Although, we have lost touch, Dad remains the best driver on the planet, not because he is my parent, but because he has proven how good he is. Now, let's leave my father aside as I have an interesting story to share with you.

On the 31st of December 2022, I drove two passengers to O'Hare. It was around noon and the streets were mostly clear. As I was approaching the terminals, I saw that the airport was empty. I slowly rolled to Terminal 1, stopped my vehicle and put the automatic shift into "Park." I had a wonderful chat with my passengers and they decided to buy one of my books (*James Dobrev: The Cold Murder*).

So, as I was signing the book, then BOOM! Someone hit me from the rear. The person didn't just hit me, but pushed my car forward, heading towards the rear of a red Rav4, which was a couple of feet in front of me. I couldn't do anything to prevent this collision. But it got worse. At the moment when this person hit me, a girl was passing between my vehicle and the Rav4. Her leg got trapped between my front bumper and the Rav4's rear bumper. The strings in my heart were pulled when I saw the girl stuck between the two cars. She was in pain, screaming. It was a horrible moment. I thought this girl would never be able to walk again. In an instant, I quickly reversed my car to free the girl who had become trapped. Fortunately, it seemed that the driver who had hit me from the rear had already moved, as I was able to back up. With caution, I reversed my car, just a little since the driver who hit me was still positioned behind me. The girl walked away. Thank God! She could still walk. So, I moved my car a bit more and stopped. Then, BOOM! The same driver hit my car, and again not just hit it, but pushed my vehicle forward, causing it to collide with the Rav4 again. It felt as though this person knew me and held a grudge against me, possibly stemming from something that had happened between us years ago. It was one of the most ridiculous car accidents that I have been in.

Jumping out of my vehicle, I saw an expensive white Mercedes behind me. The person behind the wheel was a man in his seventies. This was the man who hit me twice in just a few seconds. Anyway, I was grateful that no one got injured badly. An ambulance came to check on the girl who had her leg caught between the bumpers. She said that she was fine and didn't want to go to the ER. I was so relieved that everybody was okay. Then, the cops came over and told me that the driver who hit me had good insurance. Let me tell you something right off the bat: there is no such a thing as "Good Insurance." Insurance companies are all the same. If you are not actually injured in a car accident, they won't give you much. Now, if by any chance you end up getting some extra cash from an insurance company, you should definitely go to a casino as you can count yourself a lucky human being. On that note, I know a guy who owns a body shop. He told me once, "Insurance companies pay for parts aftermarket. They don't pay for parts that are coming from the manufacturer." I couldn't believe it, but I knew he was telling me the truth.

Bottom line: I am not saying that every senior is a bad driver. All I am saying is this: be careful when you find yourself around them. If someone on the road takes longer to respond than they should or moves their vehicle slowly, just watch out and maintain a proper distance from them. I think it is important to warn you about these types of drivers because I don't want you to get involved in a car accident. That is the whole purpose of this book.

9. Blind Drivers

Perhaps you may be asking, "What is this man talking about?" Hear me out. When I say "blind drivers" I don't necessarily mean that a particular driver literally cannot see with their own eyes. This is a metaphor that I am using to refer to drivers who act as if they don't see what is happening right in front of them. Now, I am going to prove my point. Go to my YouTube channel and watch the video called "Blind drivers 1" (https://youtu.be/FVi50j97Xqc). In this video, you can see how I slowly approached a four-way stop sign intersection. In front of me, an impatient driver in a black car attempted to make a left turn hastily. Suddenly, a white SUV approached aggressively from around my right side and proceeded straight without waiting for the black car, which was still at the intersection. The driver of the white SUV almost hit the black vehicle as they did not wait for it to pass. Fortunately, nothing really happened, but you can see how close the two vehicles were. I would categorize the driver of the black car as "impatient" since they attempted to rush through the intersection as quickly as possible. On the other hand, the SUV driver could be labeled as a "blind driver" since they failed to notice the impatient driver and proceeded without seeing them.

Another video on my YouTube channel called "Blind drivers 2" shows how scary blind drivers could be (https://youtu.be/qJjUFobV_Gc). In this video, you can see how I was driving on a side street at a moderate speed and then all of a sudden a black SUV to my right pulled out of a parking lot and almost hit me. I was forced to slow down my vehicle because the black SUV seemed not to see me. At the very last second the same driver decided to stop their car. To this day, I wonder how this person didn't see me. However, I can't say I'm surprised, as I encounter drivers like that on a daily basis.

Look at the video called "Blind drivers 4" (https://youtu.be/Wb13Yb3sG6Y). In this video, you can see how I drive slowly towards the stopped cars ahead of me. On my right side, a black Cadillac approached the main boulevard from a side street. I acknowledged the presence of the Cadillac and assumed that it would wait, as it should have. However, to my surprise, it didn't. The black Cadillac slowly kept moving forward and it seemed that the driver didn't even see me, which was ridiculous because I was right in front of them. In a split second, we almost got into a car accident, just because the Cadillac didn't want to stop as it should. Let me point this out: if the Cadillac driver had communicated with me and given a sign by flashing their high-beams, I would have let it go ahead of me. Honestly, I should let them go anyway because their approach was dangerous and could put me in an unpleasant situation, which was exactly what happened. The aggressive Cadillac driver expected everyone on the road to cater to their wishes. Blind drivers are extremely dangerous as they expect a certain behavior from others on the road. It is important to identify them and remain cautious, as they have the potential to create challenging situations.

There are drivers who don't see you or seem to be about to hit you for no apparent reason. This statement may sound ridiculous to you, but I have a short video footage that can prove my point. Look at the clip called "Blind driver, dangerous" (https://youtu.be/h9asmWLPFhM). In this video, I was driving back home after a late training session at the gym. It was around 10:00 p.m. when I found myself waiting to make a left turn on a seemingly not-so-busy street at that time. Another vehicle ahead of me was waiting to make a left turn as well. The next thing I knew, a vehicle coming from the opposite direction blasted a long and frustrated honk at the SUV attempting to make a left turn. Honestly, for a moment, I thought that the SUV would collide with the honking car. I mean, isn't that ridiculous? It seemed that the black SUV driver didn't really see the approaching vehicle. How is that possible? Again, this is why I refer to these type of drivers as "blind."

The video called "Danger in south loop" has definitely something gripping to offer (https://youtu.be/4VNUgugUwjg). While I was driving on a seemingly less jammed street, something left me stunned. A black Chevy drove on the right side of the street, which was about twenty feet ahead of me. On the left side of the street, a gray Audi decided to make a right turn, which completely blocked the way of the back Chevy. It happened so suddenly, just in a second. Fortunately, the black Chevy driver was aware and managed to hit the brakes just at the right moment to avoid being hit by the gray Audi. I must say that the black Chevy driver handled the situation professionally and can be categorized as a safe driver. On other hand, the gray Audi driver can be classified as a "blind driver" who made a foolish decision by making a right turn from the left lane, blocking the way of the black Chevy driver. While watching this video, something comes to mind: **if the black Chevy driver didn't pay attention to the road and what was happening around them, then surely that would be an unpleasant car accident.** With that being said, I have to reiterate an important concept:

it can only take a second for a car accident to happen.

Well, I am not finished. Play the video called "Another Blind driver" (https://youtu.be/mDFyvvjc-jw). So, as I was driving with a passenger on what appeared to be an empty road, suddenly a red car emerged from a side street and slowly made a right turn. It seemed as though the driver of the red vehicle didn't see me. I mean, it was preposterous. To this day, I still cannot comprehend how that person didn't notice my vehicle. Was the person insane or maybe suicidal—cannot be absolutely sure as I am not a psychiatrist. Could I ask you to do me a favor? Play the same video again and watch how slowly the driver of the red vehicle made the right turn. This brings me to the conclusion: **blind drivers can be dangerous and may put you in a risky situation.** As a safe driver, you need be aware of them as they take decisions which don't seem to align with the traffic rules.

CHAPTER 4

Sharing the Roads with Others

IF YOU DON'T PAY ATTENTION ON THE ROAD, SOONER OR LATER, SOMEONE WILL HIT YOU

Pedestrians

WALKING AT A RED LIGHT IS PRETTY MUCH THE SAME AS SWIMMING IN THE SEA FILLED WITH SHARKS

According to the National Highway Traffic Safety Administration (NHTSA) annual reports on traffic safety show that pedestrian fatalities and injuries are extremely high. In 2022, has been reported that there were 6,721 pedestrian deaths in motor vehicle crashes in the U.S. This number represents an increase of 4.9% from 2019.

This is a very important topic that needs attention. You might ask yourself, "What does he mean by that?" Nowadays, pedestrians in Chicago disregard drivers, especially in the downtown area. For some reason, they will apathetically cross the street without looking to see if a car is coming. Many people do not pay attention to the traffic lights, which is ridiculous. They are crossing the streets buried deep down in their thoughts without checking for cars. I have seen a lot of people walking on the streets as if they wanted to be hit by a car. I cannot come up with a reason for their behavior. Perhaps, some of them are suffering from anxiety, depression, PTSD, anger, etc. Those people may decide to jump in front of your car and if you're not aware of them—it can be fatal.

Please, go to my YouTube channel and look at the video called "Insane pedestrians" (https://youtu. be/5_B0SxM6yHo). The first part in this video you can see a man trying to cross the street at a red light without even looking around for approaching cars. I had to honk at him because he was crossing in front of me where I plainly had the green light. As I was passing by, I saw the man looked at me with his angry eyes as if to say, "What do you want from me, huh?" This person was absolutely combative and ready to fight me without realizing that he could have gotten run over. That being said, here is the next question: how we should respond to this aggressive and negative behavior? Just keep going and mind your business. However, if this person escalates the situation by attacking the car or banging on the windows, it suggests that they could potentially be unstable or might be dealing with a mental breakdown. In that case, I would record their behavior and call the police.

The second part is something similar, but in much more dangerous situation. I am talking about a man who was crossing a busy street in downtown against a red light and cars had to wait for him. Of course, no one wanted to run over the pedestrian, so all the vehicles waited patiently. However, it was ridiculous because the cars had the right of way. Furthermore, the person crossing the street annoyingly pointed at me as if I was in the wrong. Can you believe it? The man acted as if I was making a mistake because I waited for him peacefully to avoid putting him in the hospital. Isn't that insane? Hear me out: I don't mind this man. I don't have anything against anyone, but I think we all should follow the street rules because someone can get seriously hurt. I mean, do we all want this to happen? And then what? Lose a human's life? Lose a parent, a child with a bright future to end up at a hospital or even in a coffin? If no one takes any precautions all hell is going to break loose and people will get hurt.

The third part in that video shows a young man crossing the street without looking out for cars. I had to wait for him despite having the green light. This clip proves an important fact: **people just don't**

care. Some of them have problems in their lives and would cross against a red light without even looking out for cars. This is why it is so important to be self-aware of what is going on in the streets. All of these short videos were taken in downtown Chicago, where cars are rushing and people are crossing against red lights without paying attention to the traffic.

Another shocking video on my YouTube channel titled "The old Lady" reveals a disabled lady crossing the street on her mobility scooter (https://youtu.be/fT10UgR7bFI). While the senior lady was crossing the street a black Jeep was impatiently waiting to make a left turn. The driver didn't wait for the lady and decided to make the left turn. While making the turn, the Jeep hit the lady's mobility scooter. I was waiting at the stop sign and observed the whole scenario. It was ridiculous. Luckily, there was a police unit already at the scene. The next moment, the officers jumped out of their vehicle and approached the accident. The police had to regulate the traffic and I had to leave, but as far as I could tell, the lady looked fine. Again, this is one of the most ridiculous situations that I have witnessed. I wonder how the person who hit the lady couldn't have waited a few seconds more. What was so important and urgent that the driver couldn't wait for the lady to pass the crosswalk? Imagine if that had been your grandma or mother? How would you feel about this? God forbid. I hope that wouldn't happen to anybody.

Another bizarre situation happened while I was coming back home after a long and tiresome day. It was almost midnight when I was driving in Rogers Park. The night was pitch black. I drove prudently because my vision is not 20/20 anymore, and at that time I had not been able to see an optometrist. Anyway, so, as I was operating my vehicle I saw a green light about thirty feet away and then something unpredictable happened. I saw a young man running across the street right in front of traffic. The most ridiculous part was that the intersection was kind of busy: cars were passing from both directions. It was insane. The young man acted like a frightened deer, running in the street in panic. I cannot explain why this young person had to risk his life by crossing against a red light on a busy road; it didn't look like he was being chased by someone. Go to my YouTube channel and look at a video called "Pedestrian running at a red light" (https://youtu.be/wBggjUFU6DQ).

However, this is not the only instance where I have encountered pedestrians attempting to cross the road against a red light. I have witnessed similar situations, and to be honest with you, drivers choose to let the pedestrians pass rather than risking an accident. They prioritize the safety of pedestrians and do not want to harm anyone by running them over. To prove my point, I would suggest you to play the video "Pedestrians walking at a red light, again!" (https://youtu.be/uq6aSHTrEfA). As you can see, I was waiting at a red light on a busy street in Chicago. Pedestrians were walking peacefully in front of me, but when the light turned green, two pedestrians leisurely continued walking despite the red light without showing any consideration of it. Furthermore, these two were indifferently lost in their conversation, completely avoiding what was happening around them, as though they were strolling in a park, not on a busy street in a big city. This video is just another example of what I mentioned earlier: **people just don't care.** They walk with an attitude, as if to say, "We are walking in a crosswalk and regardless of whether we have the light, drivers must wait for us because no one would dare run over us." And the most ridiculous part is that drivers encounter similar behavior from pedestrians on a daily basis. Now, play the video called "Pedestrian showing the finger!" (https://youtu.be/Q3QydklssHc). In this short footage, I was the second car on a busy street in downtown Chicago, and just as the light turned green, something bizarre happened. A young man decided to walk through a red light, aggressively showing the finger to the drivers without apparent reason. I cannot understand the behavior of this young person, whether he is attempting to project some sort of propaganda or if he have been going through difficult point in his life. Whatever the reason may be, I believe this kind of behavior is abnormal and has the potential to escalate into an unpleasant confrontation in public. What is the conclusion here? Keep your eyes on the road, and be extremely cautious because bizarre things can happen, while you are operating your vehicle.

There is another video on my YouTube channel called "2023 pedestrians" (https://youtu.be/BXzNM530-sw). This video footage exhibits how I was waiting at the light to make a left turn. I was in downtown, Chicago at that time, and the traffic was heavy. And so, as I was waiting at the light, the green arrow indicator turned on, which meant I had the permission to proceed. As I was making the left turn, I saw people still crossing against a red light, totally failing to acknowledge me. It was as if they were sheep, but in reality, even worse, because a sheep would be aware of an approaching car. Anyhow, the people crossing the street didn't even glance at my car, as if it didn't exist. Some of them were staring at their smartphones while they were crossing the street. Apparently, they minded their business and I got that, but how can you step into a busy street on Michigan Avenue without looking out for approaching cars? What if a car were speeding down the street and couldn't stop, what would happen then? Did these people care about the ramifications of improperly crossing a street for the sake of their lives? As I mentioned before: **be aware of the people's behavior around you; whether they are in a car or just pedestrians crossing at a red light, as well as cyclists, skateboarders, or even hoverboarders.** Whoever they are—you need to be aware of them because accidents happen and people can get hurt badly. According to Google researches: on average, there are over 6 million passenger car accidents in the U.S. every year. Road crashes are the leading cause of death in the country, resulting in more than 38,000 people losing their lives each year. That said, I kindly suggest that you build the habit of learning to look around for others for the sake of your own life. Now, let's move on and dive into the next subject. Shall we?

Cyclists

According to https://injuryfacts.nsc.org, the number of preventable deaths from bicycle transportation incidents increased 16% in 2020 and have increased 44% in the last 10 years, from 873 in 2011 to 1,260 in 2020. The number of preventable nonfatal injuries increased 5% in 2020 compared to 2019.

Of the 1,260 bicyclist deaths in 2020, 806 died in motor-vehicle traffic crashes and 454 in other non-traffic incidents, according to National Center for

Health Statistics mortality data. Males accounted for 89% of all bicycle deaths, over eight times the fatalities for females.

These are scary numbers and I am sure the statistics are dead-on accurate. These facts make the problem serious, which boils down to this: **if we don't pay attention to what is happening on the road, the numbers of deaths will significantly increase.**

In Chicago, the number of people riding bicycles has rapidly increased in the past few years, especially in the summertime. Some ride bicycles to work, others do it for fun or exercise. For the most part, I see young adults and middle-aged on bikes, but also I have seen some seniors. There is nothing wrong with people riding bikes on the streets. People say: bicycles are faster. I guess that could be true; if the driver gets stuck in heavy traffic then probably the cyclist could weave their way through the traffic and get to their destination sooner. However, you need to know that riding a bicycle in a big metropolitan city such as Chicago is a huge risk. I wouldn't know that if I wasn't driving for work. What do I mean by that? Hear me out. Many cyclists think that a driver will watch out for them; that's not always the case, not every time. Drivers do not always watch out for cyclists as much as they should. On the flip side, cyclists do not seem to acknowledge this reality. To prove my point, I kindly ask you to visit my YouTube channel and play the video called "Cyclist hit by a car" (https://youtu.be/uTuF2tB7lsU). As you can see, I was driving somewhere in Logan Square area where one is very likely to encounter a cyclist. The light turned red and I had to stop at the intersection. In front of me there was a guy pedaling straight ahead and a blue car that was making a left turn from the opposite direction. Apparently, the blue car didn't see the cyclist who was just a few feet away from the car, and in the next moment, the cyclist was on the hood of the blue vehicle. It was as absurd as it sounds. The whole scenario dumfounded me. Even though I was just about to call 911, I saw that the cyclist was obviously fine, pointing out to the driver in the blue car to pull over. Evidently, the two needed to talk.

So, what is the point am I making here? This video clearly proves that some drivers are not prudent or aware of bicyclists. On the flip side, a lot of cyclists disregard drivers and act as if they own the street, expecting others to yield to them. Allow me to make myself clear. Go to my YouTube channel and look at video named "Cycling on Michigan Avenue" (https://youtu.be/NgyPNr6Uq3E). In this video, you can see a person on a bike, geared up with a delivery box on their back, rolling down Michigan Avenue—which is fairly considered to be one of the busiest streets in downtown Chicago. So this person saw the red light and decided to make a right turn, then after 3-4 seconds, the same cyclist returned to Michigan Avenue. It looked like the person was making useless maneuvers like a fly purposely hovering around. The whole scenario was something that gobsmacked me. But that wasn't all. At the moment when the light turned green, I continued on Michigan Avenue. As you can see, I was driving in the middle lane and constantly checking on the same cyclist who seemed completely unware of what was happening around them. The person on the bike changed lanes without signaling or looking if it was safe to do it. Apparently, the cyclist was lucky. However, the luck won't save them every time. You have to understand something: I didn't mind looking out for this person because I am always aware of my surroundings. The point is this— as a safe driver, I have to be aware of others around me, but that doesn't mean others shouldn't be aware of me. People on the bikes need to understand that while cycling on the road they can't do whatever they want. They need to comply with street rules and share the road with others in a safe way, or someone may get seriously hurt. This reminds me to emphasize: **cyclists need to build a habit to look out for cars just like drivers have to be aware of people on bikes.** The street rules are developed for everyone: whether that is a driver, cyclist, or pedestrian.

Let's move on and take a look at another video.

Go to my YouTube channel and look at the video titled "A dangerous Cyclist" (https://youtu.be/8pLZNOp1B88). In this video footage, you can clearly see how the sun shone straight at my vehicle and dazzled me. (Sun glare is an important subject that we will cover later on, but as for now, let's focus on this video.) So, as I was making a right turn, I had to come to a full stop because another vehicle was parked and blocking the road. Immediately, I studied the situation, recognizing the potential danger ahead. To my surprise, in the next moment, I witnessed a cyclist maneuvering between my vehicle's bumper and the left quarter panel of the vehicle in front. That was an absolutely dangerous and unnecessary move made by the cyclist. First of all, the cyclist, which was a young man, went between the two vehicles with an attitude that one could be interpret as, "Ha! Don't move! I'm just gonna go and I don't care about you." Hear me out; I don't mind this or any other cyclist, but that guy did something really stupid and perilous. Not only this but the person on that bike was a very lucky man because I was about to go, in just a second, and I didn't expect a cyclist coming out of nowhere. Oftentimes, I witness cyclists pedaling towards vehicles with dangerous speed; this is something I cannot comprehend. Why would you risk your life by rolling through vehicles who might not see you? It's like someone is swimming in a muddy bog filled with crocodiles and expecting to get away with it. I think this is a decent simile. What do you think?

Let's look into another example. Please, go to my YouTube channel and look at the video named "What a cyclist" (https://youtu.be/rr_rqlxk4zU). In this video you can see how I was waiting at a red light in the city of Chicago. As the traffic light turned green, I proceeded straight ahead. To my surprise, a cyclist decided that it was okay for them to run at a red light. At that moment, all the vehicles with a green light had to wait for this cyclist. Isn't that ridiculous? The person on the bike waved as if to say, "*Thank you!*" That was fine, but this person had made a serious mistake by pedaling through a red light. You might ask why? Here is my point: I was in the middle lane and the car next to me completely blocked the visibility on my left side, leaving me completely unable to know if a cyclist was coming at that moment. So, what does that mean? It means that I had no idea that a person on a bike was coming, and maybe only because I am a safe driver with a large amount of experience that the guy on the bike is still alive. Other drivers who might have been where I was at the video might have run over the cyclist, making a brutal accident. Here is the question that comes to my mind: why would this cyclist do something so risky? Well, perhaps this person has never been seriously hit by a car, causing them to be hospitalized for a long period of time. Don't get me wrong; I don't berate this cyclist—he is probably a good person. However, what he did that day was dangerous and something that others should learn to avoid because, at the end of the day, we are all want the same thing—to go home safe.

Look at the video called "Cyclist playing with their phone" (https://youtu.be/K-bYDJ6mKKU). As the short clip demonstrates, I was slowly driving on a side street when suddenly a cyclist almost crashed into me because they were staring at their smartphone. Pay close attention of the person's face as they took their eyes off the smartphone at the last moment, realizing what could have happened. I mean, what is the proper word to call this person? Immature? I will leave that up to you. But the next question is: how can a person ride a bicycle without paying attention to the road? **It seems that some people disregard cycling just as much as some drivers sometimes ignore driving**. Anyway. I hope this video will help you understand that people are absolutely clueless while being on the street, and are thoughtless in their actions. Now, let's look at another video that shows a good example of how a cyclist could interfere with you. Please, play the video titled "Incredibly dangerous cyclist" (https://youtu.be/jv1OJV2-FIo). In this 20-second video, I was waiting on a busy street in downtown Chicago. The traffic light turned green and my vehicle slowly proceeded with caution. The white car in front of me had already passed the intersection and I was just about to go through as well. But then something caught my attention. With my peripheral vision, I noticed a man aggressively pedaling a bicycle from the other side of the intersection. He decided to cut me off by making a left turn without looking at me. That person ran a red light and completely disregarded my vehicle by putting himself in a very dangerous position. This is something I cannot understand—why would this person run through a red light while vehicles are passing the intersection? Was he a suicidal? Maybe. The point I am making here is this: **people will keep doing those types of reckless maneuvers in front of you and that is why you need to pay a full attention on the roads, especially in busy intersections, like this one.**

Oftentimes, cyclists are hit by drivers who have parked their vehicles and, without looking out, open their doors, resulting in collisions with the cyclist. I know this is true because it has happened in front of my eyes. This is because the parking spots are right next to the cyclist's lane and this is why we should pay more attention while opening car doors in places like this. We all have to learn to acknowledge the cyclists because they could be injured badly, but that doesn't mean bicyclists shouldn't watch out for their own lives. With that being noted, I need to share a personal story with you. One day I had to use a bicycle in the city. I used one of those Lyft urban bicycles. It wasn't really a safe transportation method. I had to constantly check the cars behind me. It made me uncomfortable and unsafe. Actually, I thought that a particular car would hit me because it was too close to me. Here is my point: I watched out for the vehicles and waited at the traffic lights because I didn't want to get hit by a car and this is what every single cyclist should do. I am writing this respectfully: cyclists need to understand that they don't have any special privilege or should be treated in a special way just because they are riding bikes. On the streets, we are all equal and have to cover our backs, otherwise, people could get seriously hurt. As this goes along, an important fact comes across: **cyclists don't like hitting the brakes**. With these thoughts in mind, I have uploaded another video that further proves my point. Watch the video called "An impatient cyclist!" (https://youtu.be/xbZv1t50HYs). So, as I was waiting at a red light, an impatient cyclist came around my left side and tried to run the light without even yielding for incoming cars. Suddenly, a car rushing from across the street honked at the cyclist who tried to go before the vehicle. You can clearly see that the cyclist, a middle–aged man, barely avoided crashing into the onrushing car. For a moment, I thought it would be a collision between the man on the bike and the vehicle. It was merely a matter of seconds before a tragedy could have unfolded. The grown-up man in the video behaved like a twelve-year-old boy, and that's fine. But imagine the kind of father this man could be and the examples he would teach his kid if he acted like a middle-school student when it comes to cycling. It gives me chills when I witness cyclists taking chances, like this person in the video, and if people do not take serious precautions, more accidents may occur.

Oftentimes, I have witnessed how people on the bikes got annoyed if they have to slow down or fully stop their bicycles. I respectfully will say that this is immature behavior. Cyclists should not get mad at drivers just because the drivers have the right of way to proceed. Here is another point from my driving portfolio: sometimes I have to stop and wait for a particular passenger on a street where there is only one lane in each direction. In such situations, I cannot simply block the entire lane, as the passenger may take longer to get into my car. So, I have to partly block the bike lane, and when cyclists approach me, they get mad at me, calling me improper names. These cyclists don't understand that I don't do it on purpose rather than just trying to keep the road as safe as I can.

Conclusion: people choose biking because it is easy to move around in the city. But disregarding drivers, stop signs or traffic lights isn't safe, and cyclists must not do so, otherwise we are all in trouble. And we, as safe drivers, should be careful and look out for cyclists.

Motorcyclists

According to the National Highway Traffic Safety Administration (NHTSA), motorcyclists account for approximately 14 percent of all traffic-related deaths, even though they make up only 3 percent of all registered vehicles in the U.S.

The NHTSA notes that, year after year, "motorcyclists continue to be overrepresented in traffic-related fatalities." The same administration estimates that motorcyclists are roughly 28 times more likely to be killed in a traffic accident than people in passenger vehicles, based on the number of miles traveled. With these factors in mind, you can see that motorcyclists' deaths have been increasing over the years, and I believe, as safe drivers, we should pay a little more attention to these people. By "pay attention" I don't mean to waive at them and ask them questions or compliment their steel horses, etc. No! All I am saying is to acknowledge them and gave them the space on the road. I personally feel nervous around young motorcyclists and always let them go ahead of me because they tend to push the envelope and take too many risks on the roads. They literally play with their luck, especially those kids who don't seem to care much about the ramifications. On this note, let me share a story. One day I picked up a passenger, a man in his late forties, who was dressed like a biker. Well, it turned out that he was a biker. He was also a very friendly man. As we chatted during the ride, he told me that he had lost his leg as a result of a brutal accident while riding his motorcycle. I hadn't known that the man had a prosthetic limb as he was dressed in long jeans, effectively covering his legs, which made sense once he shared this information with me. The passenger revealed that a car ran through a red light, causing the horrifying accident. It's a sad story. This is why we all should be on the alert for motorcyclists as they share the road with others.

Scooters, Hoverboards, and the Like

Along with pedestrians and cyclists on the streets, you can encounter people using scooters, hoverboards, skateboards, etc. These people are likely to be encountered during the summertime. In Chicago, and probably the other large cities in the country, it's very common to encounter people on hoverboards, rushing through the streets. Don't get me wrong, I love hoverboards. Those mobile structures are fun and cool to be ride on. In 2021, I had the opportunity to try one out, although not on a public street. Hoverboards are a very convenient option for transportation, especially for short distances. Some of those transportation boards, like one-wheelers, can speed up to 20 mph, and that is really fast. I have seen those boards countless times in downtown Chicago, flying with surprisingly fast speed, and that could be very dangerous. Not only that, but I have studied people who were using those hoverboards on the streets, and I can respectfully say that they don't pay much attention to what is happening around them. That could be a problem because these people could get involved in an unpleasant accident. This is why it is important that we, safe drivers, need to acknowledge them. In my opinion, in near future those technologies will be more advanced and more widely used. For that reason, we should be more prudent and careful when it comes to sharing the roads with them.

CHAPTER 5

Building Driving Habits

YOU HELP YOURSELF MUCH MORE WHEN YOU HELP OTHERS

One of the most important skills any safe driver should have is the ability to create habits that will come in handy when needed and simultaneously to break those bad habits that definitely have nothing to offer. In this chapter, we will look into those good and bad habits to help you improve as a safe driver.

Stop Sign

According to Google researches national statistics reveal that 1/3rd of all intersection crashes in the United States occur at stop sign-controlled intersections, which is around 700,000 crashes annually. More than 40-percent of fatal crashes that take place every year occur at stop sign-controlled intersections. With that being said, you can clearly see that stop signs are very important and should not be disregarded. However, a lot of people do not pay attention to stop signs, especially if they are alone on the road. Running stop signs is a dangerous behavior that people should avoid. It can lead to severe accidents. This is why it is important to develop the habit of stopping at *every* stop sign. You might be asking the question: why would I stop at every stop sign if there are no cars at the stop-sign controlled intersection? It doesn't make sense, right? Wrong! By running stop signs where there is no one else around, you develop a bad habit and you most definitely will unconsciously do it when cars are present. That is why you must stop at *every* stop sign no matter what. This is how you develop a good driving habit of stopping at every stop sign.

Let me share a story with you. Back in 2010, I bought my first car, which was Mazda 323. That car ran well and it was in fine condition. I loved that vehicle, and I have many priceless memories of it. However, on one particular day, I was rolling my Mazda in my hometown, Plovdiv, Bulgaria. It was evening and the streets had already darkened. The murky night made driving difficult, but I overlooked this important detail—at that time, I thought this wasn't much of a big deal. And so, as I was driving my vehicle, my burner phone rang and I took the call. I had a quick conversation with my buddy. He told me that we could go to a party in Sofia (the capital of Bulgaria) at a prominent nightclub which I had looked forward to visiting for the past couple of years. After wrapping up the phone call, which I shouldn't have taken in the first place, I became exhilarated. Too exhilarated. The elated emotion took over my mind, and then BOOM! I found myself involved in a horrible T-bone car accident. Fortunately, no one got injured, so an ambulance wasn't necessary. Then, I realized that I was at a stop-sign controlled intersection, and it was I who was supposed to stop. I made a terrible slipup that night and I paid for it. I made this mistake because I was UNAWARE of what was happening on the road. At that time, I was twenty-one years old; a foolish and inexperienced spring chicken. But that car accident taught me a very important lesson— to keep my eyes on the road and STOP at every stop sign. At the moment of writing this, that was my first and only car accident that was my fault (besides the one where I drove the company car through a gate improperly, scratching the entire right side), but I learned a lot from it, and since then I started building the habit of stopping at every stop sign. Using this pattern, it helps me to realize how important the stop sign actually is.

Unfortunately, I don't have a video footage showing this car wreck because it happened a long time ago. However, I do have another video portraying a similar situation. Go to my YouTube channel and play the video called "Running a stop sign, bad" https://youtu.be/oyAC5ZAoT0w. It was a Saturday morning, I was going to pick up a passenger. As I was driving straight, I saw a four-way stop sign intersection. Approaching the intersection, I noticed a few vehicles going in different directions. I stopped my car and looked around. I was just about to make a left turn, but then I stopped again, watching a speeding black BMW that was coming straight at me. Looking at the rushing vehicle, I said to myself, "*This guy has no intention of stopping!*" And guess what? I wasn't wrong. The BMW disregarded the rule—the first driver to stop should be the first to go—and ran through the intersection, almost smashing into me. Let me tell you something: if I hadn't waited for that vehicle, it could have been a terrible car accident because the BMW driver was going over the speed limit and had no intentions of stopping. So, what does this video prove? It demonstrates the importance of acknowledging that other drivers may not follow the rules, emphasizes the need to watch out for their behavior and the importance of stopping at stops signs.

Now, let's take a look at the various types of stop signs located in different areas.

1. Stop Signs at Parking Lots or Small Driveways

Stop signs at huge parking lots or small driveways could be very dangerous and need to be acknowledged, just like every other stop sign. Why am I declaring this? Hear me out. It is important to pay attention to those signs because a lot of people don't and that could lead to an unpleasant car accident.

I kindly ask you to go to my YouTube channel and play the video named "Running at a stop sign" (https://youtu.be/vbn4UDF3Tjg). In this video, I was driving a passenger to a hospital, which was a huge facility surrounded by many driveways. I was on one of the driveways and slowly approached a four-way stop sign-controlled intersection, which became more like two-way stop sign situation because other drivers completely disregarded it. After I waited at the stop sign, I was about to make a left turn, but I didn't because I saw two vehicles coming from the right side. These cars absolutely failed to acknowledge where I was and ran through the stop sign without even slowing down. The drivers simply didn't care that I was making a left turn or they were too lazy to follow the rules. These drivers are the pure example of individuals who have the bad habit of not stopping at stop-sign controlled intersections. Again, this is why you must build the habit of stopping at any stop-sign controlled intersection no matter what. You also need to acknowledge that there are many drivers who tend to blow stop signs on a daily basis, whether we talk about situations happening in parking lots or other types of stop-sign intersections.

2. Stop Sign at Side Streets

The stop signs at the side streets could be quite dangerous because drivers often don't stop at them. As a safe driver, you have to look out for others and survey their behavior, especially impatient drivers. You might ask why? An impatient driver would try to beat you and go before you, even though you have stopped first and it is your turn to proceed. Look at the video called "Stop sign. They can't wait" (https://youtu.be/n75HjtCwGfE). In this video you can see how I stopped at the stop sign, on a random side street, and just before I started off, an impatient driver in front of me, made a left turn and basically took my right of way. I had no choice but to wait. However, I studied the behavior of this impatient driver and determined that they would not wait for me. In similar situations, let the impatient driver go. These types of drivers aren't going anywhere. They are not the winners. You are the winner. You have made the right decision because you are the miracle, the safe driver. You are victorious because you come back home safe. That's what it matters the most.

Let's look at another video called "Didn't Stop at

Stop sign 1" (https://youtu.be/51_CDCoz69U). It shows how I stopped at a stop sign on a small side street and just before I proceeded, I saw a black car coming from my right that completely ignored the stop sign and made a right turn. The driver didn't even acknowledge where I was standing, as they didn't care. This video is just a pure example how unware and impatient some drivers can be. Also, it showed how focused I was and how I cope with situations like this. This is why I am including the video footage. It may seem unimportant to you as nothing really happened, but if you pay close attention, you should understand the behavior of impatient or unware drivers.

Play the video called "Blew a stop sign" on my YouTube channel (https://youtu.be/efN0IIdab8g). The footage exhibits identical situation as I talked about earlier. You can see how I slowly stopped at a four-way stop sign intersection. At that moment, I was the one who stopped first and I was the one who should have gone first, but instead of moving forward, I waited because a big pickup truck, hauling a small trailer on my left side, didn't acknowledge me, and took my right of way by making a left turn. This video reveals the importance of stopping at a stop sign and waiting to see what others will do to avoid getting hit. Well, I cannot simply stop here. Look at the video called "Blew another stop sign" (https://youtu.be/

tVGu6l_rP8o). In this short clip, you can see how I approached a stop sign with a white vehicle waiting for me to yield so they could enter the street I was on. While the video may seem similar to others, pay close attention to when I stopped at the stop sign. A black SUV coming from the opposite direction completely ignored the stop sign and continued driving as if it wasn't even there. In fact, the black SUV didn't even slow down while it was passing through the intersection. The person who drove that vehicle, completely ignored everything, but their own agenda, which as you can see, was to move faster than others. The black SUV driver wasn't just an impatient driver, but in my opinion, a potential danger to others on the road. What do you think about it?

As I mentioned earlier; to avoid a car accident caused by intersection-controlled stop signs you need to develop a habit in which you make yourself stop at every single stop sign you come to. I know this is annoying and boring but if you do it, in the long run, you will see how you can automatically avoid similar situations. Again, I must emphasize this because it is extremely important: **you need to stop at every single stop sign even when there are no cars around you and you are completely alone at the intersection.** This is the key to developing the habit because if you are not stopping at intersections where you are alone, you may not do it when there are other vehicles around you. When you develop this habit, I guarantee that you will see how you are stopping automatically at the intersections where someone might cut you off and drive before you. You will stop because you have already built this habit.

The video called "Waiting at stop sign" is showing a rare moment that you may face in the future or might have encountered already (https://youtu.be/OFZW9VRGSq0). Here is the scenario: as I was driving, I saw a four-way stop sign-controlled intersection, a truck drove a few feet ahead of me, stopped at the stop sign, and then proceeded forward. On my left side, there was a black Hyundai that stopped before me at the stop sign. I also stopped at the stop sign and waited. Since the black Hyundai stopped first, I expected it to go first. But for some weird reason, the driver of the black Hyundai didn't go. I had to look at the driver and studied their behavior. It turned out that the driver of the black Hyundai was a young man who was staring at his smartphone and completely ignored that he was in traffic. I couldn't wait for this young distracted driver because I was going to pick a passenger and I didn't had any time to linger there. So, I quickly exanimated the situation and just drove, leaving the young man to play with his smartphone at the stop sign-controlled intersection. It was ridiculous. This young distracted driver had no idea that waiting at the stop sign-controlled intersection was confusing other drivers which could end up in a car accident. This is one of the reasons why the number of car wrecks has increased lately, as some people pay too much attention to their smartphones, not having any idea how they contribute to traffic in general. I will reiterate: if you need to use your smartphone so badly, then just simply park your car in a safe position to clear the traffic and avoid the confusion you may create for others.

3. Stop Signs when the Weather Is Bad

In many states in the U.S., the weather becomes bad and drivers must take extra precautions when it comes to driving. Of course, there are impatient or reckless drivers who don't care what the weather is and they will drive as fast as they can. That applies to stop signs too, especially when it snows. On days with nasty blizzards, you have to be prepared that other drivers may not stop at stop signs and most likely will not wait for you. The best way to avoid any collision with these types of drivers is to study their behavior. Again, don't stare at them or try to make an eye contact; just watch what they do. If you approach a stop sign-controlled intersection and bring your vehicle to full stop, look at the other vehicles as they may not have any intentions of waiting for you. That happens on the side streets, especially when it has been snowing for hours and the roads have not been properly cleaned. This knowledge is essential and beneficial for you, as a safe driver, and for your passengers, whether they be your family or just friends. Keep in mind that disregarding stop signs could be dangerous, and people could be seriously hurt.

Left Turns

Nowadays, the left-turn crashes have drastically increased and this is not just my opinion. Here are researches about car accidents that involve left turns:

1. An article published in the journal *Accident Analysis and Prevention* found that left-turn crashes are more likely to be severe and result in fatalities than other types of crashes. The study analyzed crash data from Florida over a five-year period and found that left-turn crashes accounted for 22% of all crashes.

2. The Journal of Safety Research found that drivers who make left turns are more likely to be at fault in crashes than drivers making right turns or going straight. The study analyzed data from crashes in Michigan over a three-year period and found that left-turning drivers were at fault in 22.2% of crashes compared to 1.2% for

straight-ahead drivers and 2.3% for right-turning drivers.

3. A report from the National Highway Traffic Safety Administration (NHTSA) found that left-turn crashes accounted for 36% of all crashes involving a crossing path of vehicles, which includes all crashes that occur when one vehicle crosses the path of another. The report also found that 94% of left-turn crashes involved passenger vehicles, and the majority of those crashes occurred at intersections.

As you can see, this information is essential, and I believe these numbers will be increasing in near future because a lot of drivers do not pay close attention while making left turns. This is why it is so important to build a habit of two major factors:

1. When You Make a Left Turn:

First thing first, watch for the drivers who are coming from the ongoing direction and second, watch for the traffic light because you don't want to get stuck at an intersection on a red light. But again, first thing, you must watch for the driver from the opposite direction as they may run through a red light. It happens all the time. I have seen car accidents where a driver, who is waiting to make a left turn, fails to observe what is happening in front of them and makes a left turn. Then, BOOM! A car collision happens because the driver making the left turn didn't wait for the one coming from the opposite direction. This is important. Hear me out: even though you get stuck at a red light and the other driver in front of you passes through the red light, you must still wait for the driver to prevent from a car wreck. I know it is a confusing concept that could give you a headache, but it is important to understand that another driver can speed through a red light, and even though it is not your fault, you still have to wait for them, because at the end of the day, you don't want to end up in wheelchair or in a coffin just because some impatient driver had decided to run a red light. With that being said, let me show you how to properly make a left turn in a very dangerous situation. I kindly ask you to look at the video called "Left turn. Dangerous 1" (https://youtu.be/y56i2zhQzLs). In this video, you can see how I slowly drove to an intersection under an overpass and waited patiently for the drivers opposite me. I noticed that the light turned red, but I didn't make the left turn because there were still cars coming toward me. This was the crucial moment where I had to realize that even though the light had turned red, I still had to be patient as the cars were still coming. Then, immediately after I was completely sure that there were no more vehicles from the ongoing direction, I made the left turn. The video shows how smoothly I did this maneuver—I have done it a million times already—but it is important to understand the concept and the point I am making here. I am doing it because I want you to became a safe driver, just like me, and avoid unpleasant car wrecks or fender benders.

Let's look at another video titled "Left turn running on a yellow, dangerous" on my YouTube channel (https://youtu.be/XTNenWUIBRM). The video shows how I calmly waited to make a left turn on a busy intersection. As I was waiting, I saw that the light switched to yellow and the flow of cars in front of me cleared for a second, but I still waited because a red vehicle from the opposite direction didn't seem to have any intentions of stopping. It was a nail-biting situation as a car behind me was honking to get me going, but apparently the driver behind me didn't see the red car coming. The moment the red vehicle drove past me, I safely made the left turn and left the intersection. This video clearly proves what should be the behavior of a safe driver in similar situations. I would suggest reconsidering the purpose of this video and replaying it a few more times. Don't just watch it once and then move on to the next paragraph—you have to realize that this video can save a lot of lives and make people aware of what is happening, because many impatient drivers won't wait for that red vehicle, and then the picture can become really ugly.

Now, the following video dubbed "Another left turn, dangerous!" exhibits a different situation (https://youtu.be/SI8b83Y4UXc). In this video, I waited to make a left turn on a street with no traffic lights. Please, look at the white car at precisely 0:00 second. As you play the video, you will notice that behind the white car was hidden a black vehicle. The white car was also making a left turn, but I waited to make sure I had a clear view of that car. After I was sure that there were no more vehicles behind that white car I made the left turn. In hindsight: this video is a vital example that depicts what you have to do in similar situations.

2. When You are Going Straight Ahead and Others Make a Left Turn.

I showed you how to make a left turn safely, but what about going straight when others are cutting you off and make a left turn? You have to be very careful when you drive straight ahead while other drivers wait to make a left turn. Watch them closely; don't stare, but shoot them a quick glance. Study their behavior: is the driver making a left turn an impatient driver? Perhaps this driver won't wait for you and will turn in front of you, or maybe they will wait for you. No one can be 100% sure until the other driver reveals their intentions. That is the key; you must observe them carefully because some of them will try to make the left turn before you pass the light, especially the impatient drivers or cocky drivers. This is why it is important to study their behavior. How can you do it? Let's dive into the next examples. Shall we?

Watch the "Insane chauffeur" video (https://youtu.be/KspFY6obQjQ). In this footage, you can see how the light turned green, and just as I was about to drive straight ahead, suddenly I had to stop because a careless driver was making a left turn and blocking pretty much the entire intersection. This driver made such a foolish mistake by venturing through the intersection. It was absolutely careless maneuver, but thankfully, nothing bad happened.

Let's look at a video called "An aggressive Kamikaze" (https://youtu.be/XRCQ2jXXouk). In this video, I was driving straight ahead at a moderate speed, adhering to the limit. Suddenly, a red vehicle decided to cut me off by performing a kamikaze-style maneuver. Even though I was prudent and watched out for the red vehicle, it still surprised me by making such a risky left turn. As you can tell, it was a matter of a second before I would have collided with the red vehicle, which reminds me once again of how serious and dangerous the streets are in present days. Of course, I am not done. The video "Kamikaze" shows identical situation where I waited at red light in a busy intersection (https://youtu.be/w2NwxNSwNBc). The next second, the light turned green and just before I proceeded straight ahead, a driver decided to perform a kamikaze-like maneuver by making a left turn and basically blocked my right of way. This video proves that there are drivers who take an extremely high risk by making left turns in front of you. This is why it is so important to be aware of what is happening around you on the roads. That being noted, something else comes to mind: **when you pass a green light, always glance at the driver waiting to make a left turn.** It is important to study these types of situations because things can get ugly in just a few seconds. Now, please look at the video called "Coming out from nowhere" (https://youtu.be/jPUAnMjGbhM). In this video, you can see how I drove straight ahead at a speed complying with the limit. In front of me there was a car that blocked the visibility which was already a sign for me to be careful. The black car in front of me made a right turn and suddenly, another silver vehicle decided to make a left turn and completely cut me off. It was insane. To this day, I still cannot comprehend why this driver made such a foolish and risky maneuver. Let me tell you something: **if I weren't driving slowly at that moment, I would have been involved in a car wreck**. Luckily, I glanced over and saw the person who had decided to take on a huge risk by making a left turn and completely blocking my right of way. He was a white man who had a very upset facial expression that alluded that he might have been in a severe mental breakdown. Now, why do I bring this up? Hear me out: life nowadays is getting more challenging, prices are sky-rocking, and people are getting angrier. That means you may encounter people with serious issues who drive incredibly recklessly, or individuals who may be feeling suicidal and decide to ram into you for whatever reason. Thus, you have to keep an eye on what is happening around you because, once you sit behind the wheel, there might be moments with other drivers that could put you in danger.

Right Turn

Right turns can be very dangerous, especially for pedestrians and cyclists. But also, it can be challenging for other drivers. Oftentimes, I have seen a collision occur between a car making a right turn and another vehicle from across the street making a left turn going in the same direction as the one making the right turn. To avoid this type of collision, you have to comprehend something important: **when you're turning right, make sure you quickly glance at your LEFT side to acknowledge the situation, as another driver may be trying to take your right of way**. But remember just a quick glance no more, as you also need to watch the road in front of you. It is particularly important to keep an eye out for impatient drivers as they may hit you while you are making a right turn. Speaking of impatient drivers, they would most likely try to go before you and often take the risk by making a foolish maneuver just to be ahead of you. This is why it is essential to watch for these types of drivers. To prove my point, I have a video called "Right turn, cutting me off from my left side" (https://youtu.be/2v5i9TLd39A). In this short clip, you can see how I was approaching an intersection. I had a green light so it was fine for me to make a right turn. However, just before I did so I glanced to my left to have an idea what was happening. Sure thing, a big SUV on my left side decided to cut me off and made the turn before me. The SUV's driver was impatient and took a risk by disregarding my right of way and cutting me off. I had no choice but to stop in the middle of the intersection to avoid getting hit by the SUV. This video clearly demonstrates what I have mentioned earlier—when you are making a right turn, take a quick glimpse to your left side because impatient drivers, waiting to make a left turn, might try to go before you. You get the point. Now, what about making a right turn at a stop sign-controlled intersection? When you are making a right turn on a four-way stop intersection, make sure that other drivers are waiting for you, especially the impatient drivers. Watch out for them because they will try to go before you, which usually can happen in the morning hours when everyone is on a hurry.

Let's look at another interesting example. I kindly ask you to play the video titled "Making a right turn, dangerous" (https://youtu.be/eBqgvLINrOM). This short video displays how I drove on a rainy day. Everything went smoothly until an impatient driver in a silver Honda decided to do a kamikaze-style maneuver and blocked my way at the very last second, just before I was about to hit the brakes as hard as I could. This snippet is just another proof of how an impatient driver disregards bad weather conditions and does whatever they want in order to be ahead of you. Remember: impatient drivers will always do something similar, and you have to learn to anticipate their annoying desire to cut other drivers off. Once again, they don't care about you, and their only mission is to reach their destinations as quickly as possible.

Another important subject that requires attention is safety around buses, especially those from public transportation. With these thoughts in mind, turning in front of buses is another problem that often can be very overwhelming. Let's face it: no one likes to wait behind a public transport bus. Why? They move slowly and seem never to be in a hurry at the bus stops, but should you cut one off, they get mad. Not to mention, it is illegal to make a right turn in front of a bus. This problem is often caused by location of the bus stop. I cannot understand why most of the bus stops are at the corner of most intersections—it really doesn't make any sense to me. If the bus stops were relocated and moved away from intersections, that could actually prevent a lot of crashes and problems that happen on a daily basis. So, what do I do when I am behind a bus at a bus stop? The answer is simple: I wait for the bus to go, and then I make my right turn. Now, if there is a gas station on the right side of the intersection, I could go through it, but only if I have to make a right and it's safe to do so. Otherwise, I would simply wait for the bus. I am driving people for work, they could be any age, and could come from all over the world—I can't afford to take the risk of turning in front of a bus and causing a dangerous situation that may turn into a collision.

Let's look at a different scenario. Please, go to my YouTube channel and watch the video "The Accident" (https://youtu.be/778FgJjO1KQ). In this video, you can see how I was slowly driving in the right lane. At that time, I was with a passenger and the GPS guided me to make a right turn into a small parking space next to Denny's. So, while I was smoothly making the right turn, then BOOM! Someone hit me from the rear. I was absolutely dumbstruck, as you might be while reading this. How the heck could someone hit me while I was making a right turn? The answer is simple: **people don't pay enough attention while driving and that's how car accidents happen**. This is why it is so important to keep your eyes on the road and maintain a safe distance from other drivers. Now, I want to point out that I didn't make the right turn too slowly to the point where my vehicle was barely moving. No! That was not the case. I made the right turn smoothly, like a limo driver would—ain't nothing wrong with that. I also want to emphasize that the person who hit us was a very respectful man. He came to me after the accident and politely asked if everyone was doing fine. This video clearly demonstrates that sometimes we cannot avoid car accidents, as other drivers around us have made an unavoidable mistake.

Traffic Lights

According to the National Highway Traffic Safety Administration (NHTSA), in the United States, about 22% of all traffic accidents are intersection-related. While traffic lights can help to regulate traffic and prevent accidents, they can also be a contributing factor to accidents if drivers fail to obey traffic signals or if the lights malfunction. In retrospect, I can say that the number of drivers who run red lights have significantly increased over the past few years. Perhaps some drivers are so obsessed with catching a green light that they end up driving through a red light because they simply fail to properly analyze the situation and put their lives and those around them in danger.

Now, let's delve deeper into the issue of illegal red light running, which occurs frequently and often leads to deadly consequences. In 2021, 1,109 people were killed in crashes that involved red light running. To avoid this, a lot of states have installed red light safety cameras. This technology is an effective way to discourage red light running. Enforcement is the best way to get people to comply with any law, but it is impossible for police to be at every intersection. Cameras can fill the void. An IIHS study found that cameras reduced the fatal red light running crash rate of large cities by 21 percent and the rate of all types of fatal crashes at signalized intersections by 14 percent.

As a safe driver, you need to acknowledge the impatient drivers and cocky drivers who tend to blow red lights. You may ask yourself the question: how can I do it? Look at the video called "Oh my God!" (https://youtu.be/9G_Thsz3J_w). This snippet shows how I approached a busy intersection. As I was driving smoothly, I saw that the light turned green so I proceeded slowly with caution. Well, I didn't go any further as a silver sedan blew a red light and blocked the entire intersection, which as a result of this, I was forced to hit the brakes in order to avoid getting into a car wreck. This video proves how some drivers would risk their lives and others' safety by running at a red light.

Another video called "Runnin' at a red light" left me speechless (https://youtu.be/CmicSETL1LI). I mean, what type of person can possibly do something like that? As you can see, I was waiting at a red light and when the light turned green an impatient driver decided that it was okay to blow a red light and rushed through the intersection, putting everyone's lives in danger. This video is a perfect example of what I was talking about earlier—sometimes people just get lucky, doing foolish maneuvers like the driver in this video and somehow get away with it. But the luck can save them once or twice—not all the time. And that's not all I've got. Play the video called "Running at another red light" (https://youtu.be/Ui_sW7e6YZ0). In the video, I saw a yellow light and immediately slowed my vehicle down. The next moment, the light turned red and after a few seconds a white truck next to me ran through the red light, causing an unnecessary frustration to the other drivers. This is just another classical example of how a driver can run a red light without any ramifications. The problem of running red lights has significantly increased over the years, and I have witnessed working-class people doing it on a daily basis. Running a red light has become almost normal these days. I have heard Chicagoans saying, "You wait three seconds on a green light, and then you go." Isn't that insane? Obviously, the next question should be: where are we going with this? And of course, I have more examples to prove my point. Play the video called "Blowing red lights on a daily basis!" (https://youtu.be/03VYcdHXP7o). Even now when I'm looking at all of these situations, it just amazes me how people can be so thoughtless or reckless to go through a red light, and leaving everyone else questioning the outcome. This is one of the reasons why I have uploaded these videos on my YouTube channel to help you understand how bad drivers could be on a normal business day. I also hope that these materials will make you a better and safer driver, the one who gets home safely.

Switching Lanes

This is definitely a very dangerous aspect because other drivers, such as impatient drivers, may cut you off by switching into your lane without considering the safety. With that in mind, there are two different places where drivers tend to switch lanes: highways and city streets.

1. Highways

Switching lanes on highways can be challenging because a lot of drivers do it improperly and abruptly without analyzing the situation. A lot of impatient and cocky drivers who think themselves race car drivers will switch lanes every second or two without considering the safety of others—it happens all the time. Please, do me a favor and play the video called "An impatient driver, dangerous" (https://youtu.be/zEa3uINdQ4U). In this video I was in the express lanes on I-90 Kennedy inbound. There was a blue car on my left side that was trying to switch the lanes and suddenly a white vehicle rushed through and almost hit the blue car, making a desperate attempt to change lanes. It was clear that the person in the white vehicle was an impatient driver who got pissed because the traffic was jammed at that moment. Drivers like this tend to make risky decisions which could put their and your own life in danger and that is happening every day, literally. It is important to watch out for them, as things can quickly turn ugly.

Some drivers may change lanes without seeing you, and at that point, you have to watch out for them. Look at the video "Changing lanes. Dangerous!" (https://youtu.be/NCWQY_3Ivd8). I was on the highway outbound towards O'Hare. The traffic was mild and cars were slowly moving. Now, pay close attention to the truck on my left side. In a matter of seconds, you'll see how this truck slowly shifted lanes, entering my lane and blocking me. As you can see, I was forced to hit the brakes because the truck was changing lanes improperly, getting too close to me. I correctly studied the behavior of this driver and realized that the person operating this truck did not see me or perhaps didn't care. Again, this isn't about being a mind-reader or making assumptions. It is about observing and studying the behavior of the drivers around you. The point I am making here is that I studied this driver correctly, which helped me to avoid getting into a car accident. I didn't honk at this unaware driver because it wouldn't have made any difference, but honking is a subject I will cover later on. What is actually the conclusion of the footage? This video epitomizes how drivers can be unaware and may improperly switch lanes without realizing how close they are to other drivers. With that being said, here comes another important fact: **as a safe driver, it is important to keep an eye on drivers next to you, that's how you will avoid getting hit**.

The video titled "Letting me go on the highway" has an important meaning behind it (https://youtu.be/VLsDlY_A5IM). I was driving on a highway with heavy traffic and needed to change to a lane where the traffic seemed to move faster. I flicked the left turn signal, indicating my intention of merging into the left lane. A black van was driving to my left, and for a moment, I thought the driver was letting me go, but they kept going. So, I looked straight at the person who was a middle-aged man and noticed that he had one eye on his phone, indicating that he wasn't fully paying attention to the road. For this reason, I didn't change the lane and waited a few seconds more. Fortunately, the man who drove that black van acknowledged me and waived, even honked, indicating that it was okay for me to change into the left lane. Remember: **indicating that you want to change the lanes by simply signaling to others does not necessarily mean they see you.** Before changing the lanes, you must ensure that the other driver is letting you to merge into their lane. Otherwise, it may cause a frustration and lead to pointless confrontation. Also, when you intend to switch lanes, make sure you watch the driver ahead of your lane, as they might suddenly hit the brakes, which could significantly reduce the distance between your vehicle and the one ahead of you. Failing to look at the driver ahead of you while switching lanes may result in your vehicle colliding with their rear bumper.

Another important subject that frequently occurs is when two drivers are coming from different lanes and merging on the same lane simultaneously. This is a very crucial concept that needs attention, and as a safe driver, you need to keep in mind the possibility of another vehicle merging into the same lane as you are attempting to enter at the same time. Play the video called "Two vehicles switching onto the same lane" (https://youtu.be/AZ_bjtLChyY). The video sports how I was driving on a highway with moderate traffic. About twenty feet in front of me was a black Jeep with a spare tire attached to the rear side. In a split second, the black Jeep attempted to change the lanes to the left, but another vehicle was merging into the same lane at the same time. Fortunately, the black Jeep driver was aware of the other vehicle and hit the brakes in order to prevent from a car accident. Remember: **when you are about to change lanes on wide highways with more than three lanes each way, make sure to look out for vehicles that may be merging into the lane you are trying to switch to.**

2. The Streets

On the streets, drivers tend to switch lanes at any moment, and if you're not careful, they could hit you in less than a second. Many drivers do not see you or simply don't care where you are or whether they are cutting you off improperly. This can be incredibly frustrating, which is why it is important to develop a habit of watching for them to avoid getting hit. That said, let's talk about how I manage situations when others cut me off improperly. Please, play video "Cut me off 1" (https://youtu.be/logaM_VAzc4). In this video, I was in downtown Chicago, driving with a passenger. Suddenly, a cab driver on my left side decided to abruptly switch the lanes and cut me off aggressively. Classical. I was forced to hit the brakes because the cab driver was too close to me. Fortunately, I avoided the situation smoothly without any frustration. How did I make it so easy? It's because I have built the habit of watching out for other drivers, and to me, it has become natural. This habit has kept me safe on the streets for a long time, and I can assure you—it works effectively.

Let's look at another video called "Cocky driver, cutting off through the lanes" (https://youtu.be/DGFm1yWWh54). In this video, you can see how I was driving smoothly on a busy street called "Cicero" towards Midway Airport. I was in the middle lane, and all of a sudden, some cocky driver operating a blue Infinity whooshed from my right side and aggressively switched lanes. I had to hit the brakes to avoid getting hit by this cocky driver. As I mentioned before: a **cocky driver might switch lanes and put you in a risky situation and you, as a safe driver, have to watch out for this type of careless driver.**

Sometimes drivers tend to make a left turn into a side street and while they wait for the cars from the opposite direction to clear out, they temporarily block the lane, causing the cars behind them to switch lanes and cut you off. Look at the video called "'Blocking a left lane" (https://youtu. be/490Cp6iMuwE). In this video, I was slowly driving in the right lane and noticed that a white car waited to make a left turn and blocked the left lane, causing the car behind it, which was a white Tesla, to make a quick decision by changing the lanes. Now, as you can see, the white Tesla didn't really cut me off. That was because I was aware of their intension and maintained a large distance from the truck ahead of me, giving the necessary space for the white Tesla to safely switch the lanes. This video demonstrates the importance of maintaining a safe distance from vehicles ahead in order to avoid abrupt interactions with other drivers.

Remember: **whenever drivers are speeding next to you and there is an empty space ahead of you in your lane, 9 out of 10 times, the speeding driver will cut ahead of you and take that empty space.** Now let's prove my point: please, play the video "Cut me off 2" (https://youtu.be/7StbGj3-ujM). In this video, you can see that there was an empty space ahead of me in my lane. The red vehicle on my right side was speeding and immediately switched lanes to move into the empty space in my lane. Once again, this isn't about being a mind-reader or anything of that nature. It is simply about studying the behavior of city drivers who, in 9 out of 10 situations, will cut you off in similar circumstances. Now, you might be asking: why am I leaving so much space in front of me? The answer is simple: by law we supposed to keep an empty space as long as three car lengths. Besides, I have to see what's happening in front of me—I can't just tailgate other vehicles. Why? Because the driver in front of you may hit the brakes abruptly and come to a complete stop, then only God would decide if you are getting away with it or not. Allow me ask you this question: why would you put yourself and your loved ones in this risky situation? Once you have answered this question for yourself, then you will truly grasp the importance of keeping a safe distance. Now, let's thoroughly discuss the topic of keeping a safe distance. Are you ready? Bear with me in the next subchapter.

Keeping Distance

Keeping a safe distance from others is crucial as it allows you to respond effectively if the need occurs. I kindly ask you to pay close attention to all of my videos, and you will notice how I maintain a safe distance from other drivers. That said, another question arises: what if a driver decides to occupy the empty space you maintain from others? If someone takes the empty space you keep from the driver ahead of you, that's fine. Don't worry about that. They won't go much further. In fact, whoever takes your empty space and keeps moving aggressively, they are pushing their luck, causing unnecessary frustration that may turn into a car accident. Perhaps they like to drive close to other drivers, thinking that they are moving much faster. This brings me to the important point: **tailgating is something that you should absolutely avoid.**

Conclusion: keeping distance is a helpful habit that every safe driver should develop. Once, you start doing it, you will realize that you actually have control over the traffic in front of you by simply maintain a safe distance from the driver ahead of you.

Visibility

Another important skill that every safe driver needs to cultivate is the ability to maintain clear visibility. What is visibility? The proper definition of this term is: the measure of the distance at which an object or light can be clearly seen and determined. Before taking any action behind the wheel, you have to make sure you can clearly see if cars are coming from at least 170 to 200 feet away for the highways and 80 to 100 feet away for the streets. On this note, something important comes to mind: **the ability to determine the visibility depends on the speed of the approaching vehicle**. What do I mean by that? Let me explain. For instance, imagine you are driving on an empty freeway and you need to switch lanes.

Again, don't just count on the side-mirror sensors as they may not detect a fast-approaching vehicle from 100 feet behind. Here comes the visibility. Having the clear visibility and the ability to study a fast approaching vehicle is the key to make safe maneuvers—whether it is switching lanes, merging, or making left turns and so on. Could you do me a favor? Look at the video called "Left turn visibility" (https://youtu.be/5wb5Bt53GOU). In this video, I drove on a busy street early in the morning when the traffic usually was heavy. The GPS guided me to make a left turn on a side street. So, I put on my left turn signal and waited on the traffic from the opposite direction. I didn't have clear visibility and waited a bit longer by moving an inch closer to have a better view of the opposing traffic and to be absolutely sure about performing the left turn. The moment when a black Ford pickup truck passed me by, I thought of making the turn, but I still didn't have clear visibility. Sure thing, a few seconds after the black Ford pickup truck had passed me, another silver car came from the opposite direction and proved that I had made the correct choice. As the silver car drove by, I moved my vehicle close enough to see if there were any cars coming from the same street. A second later, I had clear visibility, giving me the chance to make the left turn safely. It is important to emphasize that in those types of situations, you cannot rush and make your turn before the vehicles coming from the opposite direction have sufficiently thinned out, as you may end up in a T-bone car crash. Let's look at another video titled "Clear visibility" (https://youtu.be/_jNmWMgO88Q). In this footage, I was waiting to make a left turn at a busy intersection. At this moment, there were two cars waiting to make their left turns in the opposite direction, completely blocking my visibility. As I patiently waited, a black Honda Accord drove past me from the opposite direction. For a second, I thought I could make the turn, but I decided to wait. Just a moment later, a black van also passed by from the opposite direction, reaffirming that waiting for clear visibility was the correct choice. Please, do me a solid and play the video again. **This time, pay more attention to the fact that by the time the black van drove past me, the light had already turned red, which some drivers might interpret as a signal to make the left turn.** In similar scenarios, you don't complete the turn until you are absolutely certain that you have clear visibility, which would tell you if there is a car coming from the opposite direction.

In conclusion, I will reiterate what I have mentioned earlier: **before doing any maneuvers, make sure you have clear visibility.**

Peripheral Vision

Peripheral vision is definitely what every safe driver should be aiming for. The simple reason is that the peripheral vision helps you to spot other subjects approaching you, and provides you with important information about your surroundings. I would suggest you to look at the video called "Peripheral vision" https://youtu.be/2UC88U9h6us. This video demonstrates how important peripheral vision is in a real timeframe. In the video, the right lane was blocked and as I quickly changed lanes, after I was certain that it was safe to do it, I proceeded with caution, knowing that someone in front of me might want to pull into the same lane as well. Sure enough, the next thing I knew, a white vehicle changed lanes from right to left, which didn't really surprise me. Immediately after the white car, another gray Volkswagen decided to cut me off by switching lanes. I barely noticed the gray Volkswagen with my peripheral vision as the vehicle made it literally at the last second, at which I was forced to stop, as the light was about to turn red. Now, look at the video called "Peripheral vision 2" (https://youtu.be/ oRHR13Z5nHc) In this footage, I was on a highway filled with heavy traffic. At that time, I was in the far right lane, which happened to be the fastest. As a rule of thumb, I knew that someone might want to block my way and cut me off. Indeed, not too long after a white Chevy cut me off at the very last minute and I had no choice but to hit the brakes. Fortunately, I was prepared and able to avoid a potential car accident, thanks to my peripheral vision. This reminds me of another important fact: **when you are on the fastest moving lane on a highway, be very careful as others may try to cut you off**. I can't stress this enough: **the better your peripheral vision is, the safer driver you will be.** Mastering peripheral version comes with a lot of practice, but once you have it, you can only benefit from it as a driving aid that will save you numerous times while you are on the road.

Crosswalks

Crosswalks are essential part on the road that every driver should consider, especially when there are pedestrians in sight. If you're driving in a large metropolitan city such as Chicago, New York, or Los Angeles, you are likely to encounter crowded crosswalks with many pedestrians. It is important to be patient while waiting for people who are crossing the streets, whether they are at the crosswalk or about to step in. With that in mind, a video called "Didn't wait for the pedestrian" shows an interesting situation (https://youtu.be/RWfDoahQQA0). As you can see, I stopped my vehicle and waited for a mother with her little daughter, who was on a bike, to cross the street. They were almost half way across when the mother become scared and tightly held onto her daughter. She protected her child because an impatient driver honked behind me, not realizing why I had stopped my vehicle. The driver became frustrated, and tried to go around me, almost running into the mother with her daughter. At the last moment, the same driver stopped next to me, realizing that there were people crossing the street. Obviously puzzled, I looked at my left side to survey the impatient driver. It turned out that this driver was a white middle-aged man who could easily be the husband of the mother and the father of the child who were crossing the street. I have always been amazed by how a middle-aged man could act like a sixteen-year old. Not only this, but why would a man have to be so impatient as to make such immature maneuver, risking his life and the lives of others around him. This is one of the reasons why I decided to write this book and by showing the video, I want to help you grow and become a safe driver, the one who protects himself from guys like this. I must reiterate: at the end of the day, we all want the same thing—to come back home safe to our families.

Roundabouts

Roundabouts are circular intersections where vehicles travel in one direction. They are designed to improve safety for motorists, bicyclists, and pedestrians. Unfortunately, some drivers do not understand how to drive correctly in a roundabout, or just simply fail to obey the rules and cause a collision. That said, it is important to remember: **in roundabouts, you are likely to encounter various types of dangerous drivers, most of whom are impatient.** For this reason, you must watch out for impatient drivers, as 9 out of 10 times they will cut in front of you, despite your having the right of way. In roundabout-controlled intersections, you need to develop the habit of carefully studying the behavior of the drivers around you. Many times, I have witnessed situations where drivers are inches from a car accident as a result of recklessly speeding in roundabouts. This is why I must declare: **before driving in a roundabout intersection, be extremely careful, as the others around you might not be.**

U-Turns

U-turns can be extremely difficult and may create a severe car wreck. In some cases, an oncoming vehicle crashes into the driver making a U-turn because the driver miscalculated the timing of the U-turn. This reminds me to mention something essential: **miscalculated maneuvers cause unpleasant car collisions.** Oftentimes, a driver fails to do a U-turn properly, heading into oncoming traffic which causes a head-on car accident because they misjudged the situation. Other drivers make a U-turn by suddenly reversing or stopping in the middle of the road and slowly maneuvering, which can cause a car wreck with the following vehicle. Doing proper U-turns comes first with the patience and the right timing. Also, you need to ensure that everyone on the road is acknowledging your decision to make the U-turn. The video called "Making a U-turn" demonstrates how to safely perform a U-turn in a difficult scenario (https://youtu.be/P8VxjDYSIIQ). As you can see, I was on a busy road, inching my vehicle close to the lane with opposite direction and waiting patiently. I knew the other drivers wouldn't let me go just like that, and so I started communicating with them by flashing my lights to indicate my intentions. Not long after, a white van stopped to let me go. I proceeded with caution, looking at the other lane to see if it was safe to complete the maneuver. I also noticed that a blue van was waiting to make a right turn from a side street and by kept signaling, I hoped that the blue van would yield to my vehicle. After I was assured that everyone around acknowledged my intentions, I completed the U-turn. The whole process was done quickly and smoothly. However, I needed to notify everyone there of my intentions. This brings me to an important fact: **signaling to other drivers is a good method as it helps you in revealing your**

intentions. In hindsight, making U-turns can be difficult at times, and your patience accompanied by proper signaling are the keys to doing it safely.

Sun Dazzle

According to an article written in *News Leader*, sun glare causes over 9,000 crashes each year and is the second highest environment-related reason drivers get into crashes, with the first being slick roads.

As I mentioned before, sun dazzle or sun glare, is an important topic that shouldn't be underestimated when it comes to driving. Many people finish work in the afternoon hours when they are most likely to encounter a sun dazzle. Oftentimes, a sun glare may occur unexpectedly within seconds, which is enough to get you into a car accident. On that note I would recommend that you have your sunglasses on when you are stuck in heavy traffic, facing the sun. Remember the video "That was close!" mentioned earlier (https://youtu.be/9TN7JGelAJ4)? Do me a favor and play it again. You can see how I almost got into a car accident because an unaware driver got confused by the sun glare. For this reason, we all should be extremely careful when driving against the sun.

Honking

In Chicago, drivers honk their car horns pretty much

all the time and in most cases it is not necessary and even useless. Back in the 50s and 60s honking might have been necessary, but at the moment I'm writing this, it is absolutely useless, with a few exceptions which I will point out soon. Speaking of honking, in many situations, people honk because they get upset with someone who has cut them off. However, honking doesn't help them, actually, in some cases it could evoke an unpleasant confrontation and even a road rage incident. Not only that but 9 out of 10 people will ignore your honking unless you keep doing it until you get to a verbal clash with someone else, exchanging profanities that no one wants to hear. To illustrate my point, I prepared a video that clearly shows how honking can be useless in some cases. Play the clip named "Cutting me off, just now" https://youtu.be/GGaqnO9arJ4. In this video, I was driving on a side street in the city of Chicago. On my left, a blue Toyota Prius slowly cut me off and forced me to hit the brakes in order to prevent a possible fender-bender. While most drivers would have honked at the Toyota Prius, I didn't because it wouldn't have changed anything. Again, this isn't about reading people's minds. It's about the beautiful art of being a safe driver who is aware of their surroundings.

Let's look into another example, the video "Truck almost hit me at O'Hare" (https://youtu.

be/5-mEn_Lg8Cc). In this footage, I was going to make a left turn on a busy road. Watch closely what the truck on my left side did while I was turning. Did you see it? So, as I was turning and maintaining the middle lane, the same truck completely disregarded me and blocked my way in the process of turning. It was so bad that I had to veer off to the right side just to avoid being hit by the truck. Once again, honking in this case wouldn't have made any difference, except maybe creating a pointless altercation. Both examples clearly show how unaware drivers can be and honking doesn't help. You need to obliterate this habit in similar situations—instead of honking, focus on the little time you have to prevent a possible accident. Once you have done it, admire your work, because that is the beautiful art of being a safe driver, the one who knows how to avoid a car crash. Be the 10th person who successfully avoids an accident, not one of the other 9 who honked in frustration. Yes, I get it. Honking is to let someone know that they made a mistake, but so what? Honking wouldn't help you in those situations; it will cause you an unnecessary frustration and a waste of time.

Like I said before, honking in similar situations is something we all should avoid. As a safe driver, you should break the habit of honking, especially when someone is switching lanes improperly and cutting you off in a very risky way or when someone is slowly coming from a small side street and leaving you no time for reaction. With that being noted, let's break down to the situations when it does make sense to honk:

1. Cars waiting on a green light. Nowadays many drivers are playing with their phones and tend to forget that they are waiting for a light at a particular intersection. In those cases, I have to honk even if I don't want to because I can't just wait at a green light behind someone who is distracted by their smartphone. It doesn't make any sense, right?

2. When you want to let someone go onto your lane it is fine to honk, but that could be confusing to other drivers. However, I still find it to be a somewhat helpful method.

3. In situations when you merge from alleys or parking garages with no visibility it is okay to honk. If not, it is necessary to alert others that you are coming out from a place with reduced visibility. Especially if you are in a big, fast-paced city like Chicago or New York, you must honk to let the pedestrians and other drivers know that you are exiting from a garage or alley. It is actually important to be on a high alert when you exiting form a business facility or private garages in an urban area where there are

more likely to be pedestrians or other drivers nearby. Then honking is a good practice.

4. Animals. Absolutely, animals such pigeons, deer, cats or squirrels tend to jump in front of your car and it is a good option to honk at them. I can boldly say that those animals are even trained to react to car horns because they hear them often. Look at the video called "Honking at animals" (https://youtu.be/8be5U-90Vxhw). In this video, you can observe how I was slowly driving on a side street when a little squirrel ran out in front of me. I simply honked at the animal to save its life. Alerted by the honking noises, the squirrel moved out of the street. With this in mind, I have seen how other drivers drive towards animals, killing them without even looking. I am an animal lover and I believe we should all watch out for them, especially when driving. For this reason, I decided to share with you this video and show you how I managed to honk at animals, potentially saving their lives.

Speaking of animals, I remember one day I parked my vehicle at a huge Target parking lot. As I hopped out of my car, I saw a man speeding off a few feet away. This man took off so abruptly that he smashed the pigeon which happened to be on the pavement in front of him. I mean, what is the right word to call this person? I leave it that up to you. I don't have a video from that scene. However, I think it would be disturbing and inappropriate to show this situation in a video. But I do want to say that the pigeon struggled, lying out there in the parking lot, and it hit the strings of my heart just to observe the whole scenario. If Iron Mike saw this, he would probably have chased the man who smashed this pigeon. But let's leave the joke aside—if you happen to see an animal in front of you, honk at them so they can move away to a safe spot. Speaking of animals, let's dive into the next subject.

Animals on the Road

Oftentimes, animals can be found on the road, and as safe drivers, we need to acknowledge their presence. This reminds me of a story I want to share with you. Many years ago, when I was working in Michigan I had to drive to the nearest town called Muskegon for groceries. It was late at night, perhaps somewhere around midnight and the interstate was dark— no lights, just some signs. As I was driving and keeping the speed limit, the inner voice in my head said, *"Now, the only thing I need is a deer jumping out of nowhere in front of me!"* Sure enough, a few minutes later a deer jumped in front of the car. The problem was that the deer didn't just run across the interstate. No! It stayed in the middle of the freeway and stared into my headlights. It looked like the animal was drawn by the light as if Jesus was calling it to come over. Fortunately, I was driving with moderate speed and my mind was alerted that a deer might came out of nowhere as it actually did. As I mentioned earlier, honking at animals can be useful and that is exactly what I did before the deer took off.

Once again, animals such as deer, squirrels, rabbits, dogs, and cats can jump in front of you when you are driving, so it's important to be alert to this possibility and avoid a roadkill. Don't get me wrong, though. I am not telling you to stare at these animals: what I am saying is to watch the street and keep in mind that an animal can show up in front of you out of nowhere—it happens all the time.

There is something else I need to talk about. I have been noticing lately that some people love driving with their dogs on their laps. To me, this is very immature and tells me that drivers like this are not taking driving seriously and may end up in a car crash. As a safe driver, I try to keep my distance from these types of drivers because anything can happen. Even if a dog is well trained, it could still cause confusion by jumping out of the car, peeing on their owner's lap, and so on. If a dog is in the rear seat or at the passenger's lap that is fine, but having a dog sitting on a driver's lap is little too much. Don't you think?

Now, allow me to share a short story with you. I have a buddy who is a truck driver—an easy going dude from Eastern-Europe. He adopted a cat and would take it with him on long trips. One day, I asked him, "Where is your cat?" He replied that his pet had jumped out of the truck while he was on the road to Texas. He felt sad and remorseful as he had developed a close relationship with the cat. I am sure he felt foolish seeing his pet jumping out of the truck.

As I mentioned earlier, I am an animal lover, but I cannot have my dog on me while I am driving—it is too risky. It would be unfair to anyone around me having my dog on my lap while operating my vehicle. I don't want to put anyone's life in danger because of that. That is the only reason why I am writing this subchapter.

Crossing a Busy Street from a Side Street

From my driving portfolio, I can boldly say that many impatient drivers have a tendency to cross busy streets without properly analyzing the situation and may come from out of nowhere. I think this is a very important topic that should be taken seriously. With that being said, let's look at the video called "Coming out of a side street" (https://youtu.be/GVhNJ8-Sys8). The video shows how I was driving on a two-way, with traffic in each lane. In front of me, a black SUV came out from a side street, and without proper consideration of the surroundings, made a risky decision to cross the street. Not only this, but the black SUV didn't have proper visibility, indicating that the driver was unexperienced or was just being cocky. As you can observe, a yellow vehicle, coming from the opposite direction, almost crashed into the black SUV. It was a miracle that these two vehicles didn't collide, which proved how lucky some drivers can get at times. As I said earlier: **luck can save them once or twice—but not all the time.** This statement reminds me of the phrase: **just a single mistake on the road can be fatal.** Please, do me a favor: I would ask you to rewind the video again. Pay close attention and look at the distance I was keeping from the vehicle in front of me. I always maintain a long distance for that purpose, to be aware of what may happen while I am driving.

The clip titled "Crossing a busy street part 1" features a simple footage of how I crossed a busy street (https://youtu.be/zfYFh60sTSo). As you can see, the key to doing it safely and properly is just be patient and wait for the other drivers. Even though it looks easy, I avoid doing it because crossing a busy street requires calm and patience and those are qualities that not many drivers have these days. With that in mind, the point I am making here is this: **a**

patient driver can become impatient if they have to wait for a long time to make their move. Crossing a busy street from a side street is the situation where a patient driver could transform into impatient driver. For this reason, I possess tremendous patience when it comes to crossing a busy street from a small side street.

Potholes

Potholes are difficult hindrances as their size can damage your tires or suspension of your vehicle. While the most outskirts have barely any of them, large cities have all sizes and shapes you could imagine.

Potholes can be annoying obstacles on roads, perhaps the same as police troopers, which all drivers tend to avoid—while it may not sound the most eloquent simile, it does strike as being quite accurate. Don't you think?

Avoiding potholes is undeniable and even necessary for the sake of our cars and smooth cruising. For that reason, as a safe driver, you need to learn how to avoid them properly and safely. What do I mean by that? I have seen many instances where drivers abruptly veer out of their lanes in order to avoid potholes, taking a risk and almost crashing in doing so. Avoiding potholes abruptly could cause an unpleasant frustration between drivers which may escalate into a road rage. This concept stumbles upon a major topic: **it is vital to avoid potholes smoothly and make sure you won't interfere with other drivers while doing it.** Throwing a quick glimpse at the road and acknowledging potholes, checking both of your sides to ensure that the driver next to you is at a safe distance, then you can drive around the potholes safely—this is what a safe driver does. It takes time to acquire such an important skill. But, don't get discouraged. As long as you put effort into learning this method, it will come to you naturally. The moment when you say, "I can't do it anymore. I'm sick of it!" is the moment when you should be putting in the effort to learn this skill. As a Chicago driver, it took me about two years of consistent practice before I learned to avoid potholes safely, but that doesn't necessarily mean that it will take you the same amount of time. With this in mind, I have to declare: we are all different. For this reason, we all respond to education materials differently. However, the important fact here is what I mentioned earlier: **just keep practicing it and it will come to you naturally.** That's what matters.

Speed Humps

Speed humps are designed to slow down excessively speeding drivers on side-streets where children may be playing. These road obstacles serve their purpose effectively, but it has come to my attention that many people, who are in a rush to get to work early in the mornings, often fail to pay attention to the speed humps and drive over them quickly, which can potentially cause damage to their vehicles. For this reason, I uploaded the video titled "Speed hump" on my YouTube channel (https://youtu. be/5uy41BFrzxk). This video footage shows how I drove on a side street while a red vehicle in front of me completely disregard the speed hump and ran over it as quickly as possible. It passed over the speed hump so quickly that, for a moment, I thought it would hit the bottom of the vehicle. Thankfully, nothing serious occurred, but this video serves as a good example of how some impatient drivers react in such situations. As you can see, I also drove over the speed hump quickly because I had to pick up a passenger. However, I still took the speed hump seriously and took a moment to slow down and drive over it safely.

When approaching a speed hump, there isn't much to do other than slowing down your vehicle and allowing it to drive over the bump smoothly. As a safe driver, it is important to remain vigilant and be on the lookout for speed humps while driving on side streets. At the end of the day, driving quickly over speed humps won't get someone to their destination any faster. So, why would anyone take the risk of damaging their vehicles for the sake of passing swiftly over a speed hump? It makes no sense, right?

Road Rage

Road rage is something that we all should absolutely avoid—it is not worth it. With that being stated, this comes to mind: **no one needs to fight on the road under any circumstances.** Usually, people who tend to start fights have some sort of problem in their lives: a mental breakdown, issues with family, stress at work, poverty or divorce, and so on. As I am writing this, I can see that road rage is becoming more common when there is inflation and the prices of everything are skyrocketing. This makes people upset and often that can lead to a road rage. This is a problem that occurs on a daily basis, and it seems to be escalating as I hear in the news of people being shot in road rage incidents.

As a rideshare driver, I absolutely avoid any road rage, especially when I have passengers with me. It looks bad for the business. I mean, I wouldn't want to be in a car where the driver freaks out every five minutes or so, jumping out of their vehicle to scream at other drivers. I also have noticed that many people tend to get frustrated over petty situations, which may escalate into something bigger. This reminds me to emphasize: **don't let your emotions take over your driving behavior.** Following this thought, let's talk about how to bear with situations when some driver pisses you off. First things first, do not do anything that would increase your anger. If someone blocks your way, cutting you off in a nasty way, just take a deep breath, then slowly exhale. Then repeat this cycle again and again. Once you start doing it, you will notice that your frustration will subside. As you continue to repeat the cycle, you will feel the difference. While you are engaged in this process, it is also helpful to grip your steering wheel tightly—if you are strong like Dwayne "The Rock" Johnson maybe you shouldn't hold the steering wheel as you might detach it from the car. Joking aside, inhaling and exhaling slowly is a good enough process. All you need to do is to keep repeating the inhaling and exhaling cycle, and then the sudden burst of outrage will dissipate. Develop this habit, and you will see the outcome—it helps a lot. Don't get me wrong; I am not saying that I never get upset by some driver making a foolish mistake on the road and putting everyone around in danger. What I am saying is that the use of breathing techniques will most definitely help you to calm down without much frustration. Could I ask you to do me a favor? Next time you are on the road and someone upsets you really bad, just hold your breath for about 10 seconds and slowly exhale. Then, do it one more time, and you will tell the difference. It certainly takes some time to break this habit. But as long as you keep doing it, you won't believe how beautifully it works to reduce frustration and anger.

The next logical question should be: what do you do if someone attacks you while you are in your vehicle? As I mentioned earlier, in case someone attacks you while you are waiting in your car, you should immediately lock yourself in your car and shoot a video of the person. Make sure you have the assaulter's face on your phone and call the cops immediately. I hope this piece of advice will help you as I pray you never get into such a situation.

Carrying a Gun in Your Car

To me, carrying any type of gun or other weapon is definitely not a solution to anything, and I wouldn't recommend it. A weapon in your car can only escalate a problem that you should avoid. Of course those who love guns, hunting or just going to the shooting range would disagree with me, and I am cool with that. Here is an interesting fact: as I write this, I drive for work in Chicago daily for six to eight hours and have never needed to use a gun, despite the drastic increase in shooting incidents in the city over the past few years. Unless you are a cop or some other law enforcement official, carrying a gun in your car is definitely not a good option. Of course this subject is ultimately and absolutely your choice. It is important to acknowledge that I am not trying to tell you what to do, I am just sharing with you my honest opinion. Here is an interesting quote from Jim Carey: "Don't hide a gun in your glove compartment because if it's there, sooner or later you're gonna use it." I do believe that these words carry a profound meaning. What do you think?

GPS

GPS systems have been available in cars for 30 years, and today people (including me) use it consistently while driving, just as we all use our legs to walk. This gadget is so convenient that it has become part in our lives. However, if you don't use it properly, it may turn into a nightmare. As I mentioned earlier, overusing the GPS while you're driving can put you in an unpleasant situation. For this reason, it is vital to use it reasonably, and avoid staring at it longer than a second. As I mentioned earlier: **if you ever get distracted or confused by your GPS, just pull over somewhere in a safe spot and take your time to figure out where you need to go.** I have encountered so many distracted drivers while they are trying to understand where their GPS is guiding them. GPS distractions will happen to anyone who is unfamiliar with the area they drive into. This is not really a secret to anyone. It is very annoying when someone in front of you drives too slowly and seems not to be paying enough attention to the road. We have all been there. I still remember the days when I started driving in downtown Chicago. It was a nightmare and difficult for me while using GPS and not having any idea where I should be going. There were moments when I had to stop somewhere in a safe area just to check where the GPS guided me. No one taught me how to drive in Windy City. GPS was actually the only guidance I had at the time, and I am still using it to this day.

Dash Camera

If you drive at least two times daily, whether to work or running errands, I would suggest buying a dash camera (if you don't already have one). Dash cameras have become a useful tool in the digital era. Why wouldn't they? You can only benefit from a dash camera, especially in case of getting into a car accident and the other driver is blaming you when it is clear that they are the one who is in the wrong. In many fender-benders, police refuse to come on-site, suggesting that you go to the nearest police department and file a police report within the next seven business days. In those cases, your dash camera will show exactly what happened and you won't even have to explain—the police officers will immediately get the memo. This statement brings an important note: **your dash camera is your best witness.**

I have been using my dash camera for about four years, and I don't regret a penny I spent on it, as I have encountered various situations when it saved me. On that note, a story from my driving experience takes me back to the spring of 2021. At that time, I drove in Park Ridge, which is a neat neighborhood near the city of Chicago. It was around noon on a rainy day when I received a rideshare request nearby. As I drove on the streets of Park Ridge, suddenly a police vehicle tailgated me and turned on its lights, indicating that I had to pull over. I was puzzled by the police as I kept to the speed limit and had acquired all the stickers required to operate my vehicle. However, I obeyed the law enforcement and pulled over. A few seconds later, a police officer knocked on my passenger's side window. I looked at the officer and saw a man nearly my age. Then the trooper asked if I knew why he had stopped me, to which I simply responded with a no. The man said, "I see now you have it on, but a block away you haven't buckled your seatbelt." I was shocked by his words, but then realized that the officer was messing around with me. I then quickly responded, "Sir, that's not true and I can prove it," pointing at my dash camera. The officer squinted at me and declared, "Okay, if you prove me that you had your seatbelt on in your camera recordings, I'll let you go without a ticket." I agreed and briskly took my camera, searching for the video that was taken seconds before the officer had stopped me. My dash camera was set up to record every five minutes, after which it would start another recording for an equal duration. Imagine how many five-minute videos it could make in about eight hours of driving. For that reason, I needed more time to find the specific video. Since the police officer had messed around with me by throwing false statements regarding my seatbelt, I decided to play with him too. What do I mean by that? I simply made him wait me for about six to seven minutes in the rain until I found the particular video. It got to the point where the police officer got frustrated, asking me to hurry up, as he had gotten soaking wet from waiting in the rain. I waited a little more and showed him the video I was looking for. After a quick examination, the police officer agreed that he had made a mistake and let me go. But it wouldn't have happened if my dash camera wasn't there. This is just one of the moments when my dash camera saved me. There were a few other moments where I needed to show the police a minor car accident that had transpired the day before. With that being noted, the next question arises: what kind of dash camera you should buy? There are several different brands that I believe are competitively good. However, the one that I am using at the moment I am writing this, is called "Vantrue N2 pro." To be honest with you, I can't really complain about my Vantrue N2, with the only exception perhaps being that this dash camera needs manual formatting in every 4-5 days to ensure its proper functioning. At the end of the day, I am sure that whichever brand you choose will be worth the money.

Parking

Parking can be frustrating, especially when you are in a big city where there aren't enough vacant parking spots available on the streets. Oftentimes, I notice that a driver will leave their vehicle where it blocks the road, which makes it difficult for others to pass by. Look at the video titled "Improper parking" (https://youtu.be/4SC6eYqQCKk). This video exhibits how I was driving through a side street and in front of me a van stopped at the intersection in a way that not only confused, but also kind of prevented me from making a right turn. In this case, I had to look at the driver to study their intentions and make sure that they were acknowledging me while I was making the right turn. Fortunately, nothing happened, but I was on the edge while I was making the right turn. In this moment, this driver's most appropriate behavior would have been to put on their hazard lights, which would have indicated what their intentions were, and then backed up as much as possible to clear the intersection so that others would not worry. Perhaps this driver was thinking, "Why do I need to back up? There is enough space to go around me!" My answer would have been: because other drivers need to know that it is safe to go around you, without worrying about getting into a senseless car accident. Now another question may arise: what about the crosswalk? Then, blocking the crosswalk would be fine because there were no pedestrians in sight. Let's look at the next possible scenario: what if there were pedestrians, especially disabled people who may have been using mobility scooter? That would have explained why the van-driver parked like that from the get go. With that being said, here comes another important phrase: **every situation on the streets is unique and can be interpreted based on the surrounding circumstances**.

Now, another point that needs attention is overnight parking, especially in large cities. If you need to leave your vehicle in a big city, make sure you park it on a side street. Avoid leaving your car parked on a busy street overnight, as there is a risk of finding it severely damaged the following day. That is one of the worst nightmares that any driver can face. Just imagine you step out of your building on a regular Monday morning and discover your vehicle brutally smashed on a busy street where you have left it the night before. It is not your fault since you didn't do anything wrong, but your vehicle is damaged. What do you do next? Contacting your insurance company might be necessary, but that could mean paying a deductible. Additionally, many insurance companies tend to increase monthly premiums unless you have a spotless driving record spanning over 20 years or accident forgiveness coverage. With these thoughts in mind, the conclusion breaks down to this: **avoiding overnight parking on a busy street can save you a lot of stress and money.**

Speaking of overnight parking, I have an interesting story. So, one particular Monday, just before publishing this book, I drove back home after training at the gym. It was around 10:00 p.m., and the street where I lived had no empty spots. For this reason, I was forced to leave my vehicle by a public park district area, which was a block away or a 2-3 minute walk from my crib. The following morning, I went to my vehicle where I left it the night before, and as I was walking, I realized that my car was gone. It was clear that the vehicle was stolen. And so, I immediately called the police to make a report and informed my insurance company about the bizarre situation. It goes without saying that my vehicle was a Hyundai Sonata, implying that whoever took the car had watched the infamous Tik-Tok video which went viral a few months ago showing how to steal Hyundai or Kia with a phone charger. To make the long story short, the police found the car four days after the theft. The car looked so bad that the insurance adjuster, after conferring with a local body shop, told me it would be a write off. Sure I get the check, but I lost the car with which I made my living. And that has put me into a difficult situation. So, what is the point of the whole story? I wouldn't recommend you buy a Hyundai, or if you do, make sure that your vehicle is well secured with an additional alarm or steering wheel lock—something I should have done. Otherwise, it could be easily stolen.

Signaling

Proper signaling is important when it comes to driving. As a safe driver, you need to develop the habit of signaling at the right moment to avoid any unnecessary frustration. That said, allow me to ask you this: how annoying is it when a driver decides to block the lane by making a left turn into a side street and signals their intentions only at the very last moment? You don't want to become that type of driver, so I would suggest that you always signal your intention of making a turn at least 50 feet before the turn. By doing it so, you won't encounter someone behind you honking in frustration. But wait a minute: what if you have to do a left turn spontaneously and give a signal at the last moment? Of course, no one can stop you if you have to make a left turn at the very last moment. However, I would give you this piece of advice: if you know that you have to make a left turn spontaneously, then drive slowly so the driver behind you will have the time to respond. Don't just drive at a high speed and then at the last minute hit the brakes causing your vehicle to come to a full stop, and then signal to make a left turn, as the driver behind you may stop right on top of your bumper. You may say, "Yes, but it's the other driver who made a mistake and they should be held accountable for the collision." To this question, I would answer with this: do you really want to get involved in a situation like this? As I said it before; this book is designed to help you become a safe driver. That is my only purpose.

Now, signaling is also helpful when it comes to letting someone go, whether by flashing your lights or honking. It is good to give your permission and let other drivers know your intention by signaling, as they may be wondering about your choice. As I mentioned this, something important comes to mind: **signaling is an option between drivers that helps them communicate.**

Road and Traffic Signs
Failing to follow or disregarding road and traffic signs may result an unpleasant situation or even a car

wreck. That of course may come across as a cliché and sound annoying to you, but from firsthand experience, I can tell you that traffic signs are very important and the roads can turn into hell without them. Furthermore, signs are placed on purpose, helping us by telling important information regarding the roads. As a safe driver, reading signs is a must, especially "Wrong Way" or "One Way" signs, and of course, speed limit and stop signs are extremely important. But that doesn't mean that other signs are less important. Construction signs, for instance, tell us a lot of useful information such as indicating a detour if the road we are on is closed ahead of us. Building the habit of reading road and traffic signs is essential because they will help you become aware of what is happening around you. This is a helpful formula for being a safe driver. On that note, impatient or distracted drivers who misread road and traffic signs may become dangerous obstacles, which is something that you may come across as you spend more time on the roads. Also, traffic signs are crucial when it comes to what you can or what you cannot do when you are stuck in heavy traffic or a difficult situation, questioning yourself about what you should do at a particular moment. Following these thoughts, an interesting story from my driving introspection comes to mind. Look at the video called "Confrontation" (https://youtu.be/fjmUS0J4xGw).

I was driving a female passenger to work from the South Loop to the north side of Michigan Avenue in downtown Chicago. The female passenger expressed her aggravation of being late for work and I tried to help her. The GPS guided me to hit Inner Lake Shore Drive, and as I took it, I didn't see a sign that might forbid making a U-turn, so I decided to give it a shot. I patiently waited for the cars coming from the opposite direction and began doing the U-turn. I had to perform two maneuvers since the street didn't offer much space, but I could do it because no one was coming from behind. As I made the U-turn, the female passenger got angry and told me that we could have gotten into a car accident. I was like, "How does she come up with this statement when no one was behind us, and I performed the U-turn quickly and safely?" The passenger didn't agree and left the vehicle by slamming the door with frustration. Later on, the female passenger filed a complaint, and the people running the rideshare platform I used, contacted me regarding this unique situation. I explained the entire scenario and sent them this video as a proof. The people managing the rideshare platform studied the video and came to the conclusion that I wasn't wrong, but for the future I should not be making such risky maneuvers. I absolutely agreed with them and that was the end of the conversion. Now, why am I sharing this story with you? This particular situation helped me to understand something vital. I said to myself back then, "Why would I need to do this type of maneuver and create unnecessary frustration? Instead, I should have done a left turn and gone around the block. So what if we arrive at the destination two minutes later than initial ETA. Would that change anything? Absolutely not!" The point I am making here is: **don't make risky maneuvers (like what I did in this video in particular); just take whichever road looks easier to you.** Don't risk getting into a car wreck by making difficult maneuvers just to save a minute or two, considering that those extra minutes you may have spent later on something petty. It is not worth it.

Another important note needs to be emphasized here: **sometimes there may be a tree or other objects obscuring the traffic signs**. This can be very dangerous as it makes the signs difficult to be read. The stop sign, in particular, is one of the most commonly obscured traffic signs that can be encountered, especially in small intersections. Ergo, it is crucial to remain highly vigilant when approaching intersections on side streets.

CHAPTER 6

Driving in Different Areas

DRIVERS SHOULD ALWAYS PAY ATTENTION ON THE ROAD NO MATTER WHERE THEY GO

In this chapter, I will discuss what it is like to drive in different terrains and types of roads. I will also break down the challenges in each area and examine the unique considerations involved when driving in them.

1. Highways

Driving on a highway can be very challenging and there are a few attributes that you should consider. First and foremost, the traffic on highways can change in a matter of seconds. Have you asked yourself the question: how come the highway was empty a minute ago and now I'm stuck in a heavy traffic? It could be a car accident where every passing driver has to slow down and stare at the collided vehicles. Or it could be construction where one or more lanes are closed. But in Illinois, and I guess in other states too, there are situations where the highway is relatively empty, then all of a sudden severe traffic happens out of nowhere, causing you to slow down your vehicle, and then some minutes later, the highway clears without any apparent reason. There is a brief period of time between driving on an empty highway and encountering heavy traffic which must be recognized. Otherwise, it may be too late, and you may find yourself hitting on the brakes, slowing down your vehicle as the cars ahead of you have come to a sudden stop. To make things more interesting, I uploaded a video called "Changing traffic on a highway" (https://youtu.be/ipdlFregw8o). In this short clip, you can see how I was driving on a clear highway where there was no traffic. As I usually do, I was keeping a safe distance from the car ahead of me, which at that time, was a white taxi. But unexpectedly, the distance to the white taxi had reduced significantly, and I found myself hitting the brakes severely, forcing me to a complete stop just in a few seconds. Isn't that insane? Not to mention, the vehicle behind me, which happened to be a big rig, had to struggle and hit the brakes forcefully to avoid crashing into my vehicle. This is why it is so important to keep your eyes on the road and avoid any sort of distractions. Why am I telling you this?

Because on a highways everything may happen in a split second. This fact brings up an essential point: **the traffic on the highway may change in a blink of an eye.** Again, this is why it is so important to keep your eyes on the road. As this point goes on, another important fact comes to mind: **every time you take your eye off the road, the risk of a potential car accident significantly increases.** For this reason, I suggest you avoid staring at your smartphone while you drive on a seemingly empty highway. Otherwise, you may find yourself hitting the brakes to prevent a potential car crash. With these thoughts in mind, another important fact needs to be specified here: when you see traffic ahead on a highway start slowing your vehicle down from a distance. Don't just hit the brakes when you are already too close. By reducing your speed from a distance, you allow your car to cruise smoothly and give yourself enough time to react if any impatient or cocky driver decides to swerve in front of you. Why am I saying this? I am not telling you this because I want you to read my book and make money out of it, but to share important knowledge, as I have done it thousands of times already. Allow me to explain. There are mainly two kinds of drivers that you can encounter on the highways: passive and active drivers. Passive drivers are those that choose to cruise at a specific speed and usually stay in the same lane. They seem to be no in a rush and are complacent to follow the speed limit, which may come off as annoying at times. On the other hand, active drivers, that is, cocky and reckless drivers, are quite the opposite. They change lanes every second or two, and seem to speed as much as possible. Your goal, as a safe driver, is to recognize these drivers, so you can stay away from them and keep your journey safe.

There is something else I need to point out: when the highway is pretty open and cars are rushing, don't drive in their blind spots. Try to avoid this because other drivers may not be aware of you and once again the blind spot censors don't work well enough all the time. Also, avoid being next to big commercial trucks, and don't drive in their blind spots either. I have a few buddies of mine who are truck drivers and they always express their frustration about how the sedan-drivers are rolling on their blind spots and how annoying that can be. One more thing, don't drive behind big commercial trucks on highways. Why? First and foremost, they mask your visibility and that may be a problem for you. Second, a truck might kick up a small rock into your front windshield, damaging it. When a small crack appears on your front windshield you should immediately go to AutoZone or O'Reilly Auto Parts and buy a Windshield Repair Kit. It's a glue that fills the little crack on your window and prevents it from getting larger. You might be asking: how to apply it? Just follow the instructions in the kit—it is not that hard. If I can do it, so can you.

I remember the first time a small rock hit the windshield of my car. It made a small crack that could barely be seen. It had never happened to me before, and I thought, "*Well, It's not a big deal. I can hardly see it!*" Sure thing, it was true enough, but after a few months the crack expanded over my entire windshield and I ended up having to replace it, which meant paying a significant amount of money. After that, it happened that my windshield got cracked two more times because I was driving behind commercial trucks. But when I bought the Windshield Repair Kit and followed the instructions, the crack never got bigger and I didn't have to replace my windshield.

Now, let's discuss some bizarre cases where certain drivers act in completely odd ways, which can be confusing for others on the road. To illustrate my point, I happen to have a video called "Stopping on a highway," which offers something even more interesting (https://youtu.be/QiOI6HoQuM0). As you can see, I was on a highway with heavy traffic. Suddenly, a black Tesla in front me decided to push the hazard lights and basically blocked the entire lane for whatever reason. Observing the black Tesla, I was speechless, as I had never seen such rude and selfish behavior on the road. The black Tesla driver could have pulled into the emergency lane, but instead they blocked the right lane, making everyone, including myself, pissed. I had to wait for a few seconds because the drivers in the left lane didn't let me in. However, after a few seconds more, I managed to pull around the Tesla. I couldn't help but wonder who the person behind the wheel of that black Tesla was. As I drove past, I saw the driver, a white man in his late thirties, completely disregarding what he had done and staring at the monitor of his dashboard. Don't get me wrong, though; if the black Tesla has broken down and become undrivable, I would have understood his actions, as the person may not have had many choices in that situation. But it appeared that the guy was simply confused by the GPS of his vehicle. In fact, you can see that he continued driving, just seconds after I managed to switch the lanes. Isn't that insane? Honestly, I have never seen anything like that on the roads. This video proves once again how unware and selfish people can be. This is why we need to pay attention and keep an eye out for those types of drivers.

Let me share another story. Back in 2011, in my country of birth, Bulgaria, a friend of mine invited me to his parent's house a few miles out of town. So I took a few buddies and we drove out there. At that time, I was twenty-two and partied like a rock star. Anyway, the weekend was over and it was time to go back to the city. It was then that I made a very important decision. I went to take a nap because I wasn't okay to drive. A couple of hours later, I woke up and with my buddies we headed to the city. I was driving on an interstate road with one lane in each direction. Just a few miles before reaching the city, I saw a blind turn about 120 feet ahead of me. Suddenly, a large commercial truck appeared from around the blind turn and was soon driving onto my lane. The truck was coming at me with speed exceeding the limit. So, I had just a few seconds to decide on which way to go. If I had gone into the left lane, I might have rammed into another vehicle, which didn't appear to be a safe option. So, I decided to turn the steering wheel to the right to avoid getting hit by the oncoming truck. Next thing I knew, I was in an ambulance, heading to some hospital. I had to spend a few days there, but thanks to the Lord Almighty, I had only a broken chin. Later on, I went to see my vehicle. I couldn't recognize it because it looked like a metal art sculpture. As I peeked through the driver's side window (where I was at the moment when the car accident occurred), something caught my attention. I saw the gas and brake pedal area had been brutally smashed. Then, I came to a horrifying conclusion: I had no idea how my legs remained untouched—it was a pure miracle. After this major car accident, it took me some time to get into a car again. I feared to be in a car as a passenger. As for driving, I thought I would never sit behind the steering wheel again. Today, as I am writing this, I am a rideshare driver who makes a living from driving. This is the purpose of this book—I have come from a place where the trauma and the pain from this car accident almost killed me and I want to help you become a better and safer driver because I don't want you to experience the suffering I went through.

As a rideshare driver, I often have conversations with passengers who happened to have similar experiences. They tell me that they feel a tremendous fear of driving because of the trauma they have endured from being involved in a severe car accident, just like me. One man, whom I have spoken, had his leg fractured as a result of a car wreck, and he would be walking with a cane for the rest of his life. That is a huge turmoil to be dwelling on. This is why we should not take driving for granted and take a moment to consider the potential consequences of being involved in a car crash.

Now you know my story and where I have come from with my tragedy, but here I want to point out something that is just important as my story above. Please, go to my YouTube channel and play the video titled "Cutting me off at the ramp" (https://youtu.be/iAZt-fQFliM). In this video, you can see how I was exiting the highway, when all of a sudden, at the opening of the ramp, a white SUV decided to cut in front of me by driving slowly but dangerously close to my vehicle. I was forced to reduce the speed of my vehicle because the white SUV was coming towards me. Technically, this driver could be classified as a "blind driver," judging by the way they approached me. As you can clearly see, the SUV driver wasn't aware of me and rudely blocked my way. Thankfully, the driver made this mistake while driving slowly, so I had time to react without coming to a full stop. Now, here is why I am emphasizing the importance of being aware of other drivers around you.

You see how dangerous entering an exit ramp can be, but what about a long road trip. If you ever happen to be on a long trip, make sure that your car maintenance is updated: tires, battery, oil change, and so on. Also, it is always good to have a portable air compressor in your car, because long trips can cause damage to your tires, even if you have replaced them before deciding to go on a road trip. I believe AutoZone has them for 40 bucks.

I vividly remember when my ex-wife and I decided to move to Dallas, TX. She had gotten a job offer, but her new employer wouldn't pay for moving, and so we embarked on a trip from Chicago to Dallas. At that time, my ex-wife had an Infinity Q65 model 2011—a big, luxury car. She decided to use her car as a U-Haul truck and loaded it with a bunch stuff that she didn't need. I told her that we should hire a moving company to do the rest of her baggage, but she refused to listen because she was a very stubborn person. Anyway, we loaded the Infinity with everything we could fit in and her beloved dogs and hit the highway to Texas. What can I say—an American Dream. It was the most bizarre trip I have ever been on. Our first stop was Mattoon, IL, my wife's hometown. The next day, I drove ten hours straight. Needless to say, we stopped about every two hours or so for her puppies (two miniature cocker spaniels) to do their business. On that trip, my ex-wife didn't drive and that was fine with me, but when it came to the point that I needed to rest, we found a place to spend the night and took our time. This is the point I am making here—**if you ever happen to go on a long road trip, take your time and rest as much as you have to**. Don't be a hero and push the envelope, because when you are tired your reactions become slower and your ability to analyze situations with other drivers can change. Remember: **a single mistake could cost you your life or that of the people around you.** On this note, I have another story that requires attentions. Back in 2015, I was working in construction and had to drive over 50 miles each way to work. After we wrapped up for the day, I would jump in my vehicle and drive back to my place. On the way home, I fell asleep a few times, causing my vehicle to swerve into the other lanes. Literally, I was falling asleep as if I suffered from narcolepsy. Fortunately, nothing ever happened, but it made me very nervous. After that day, whenever I felt sleepy I would just drive into some random parking lot and snooze in my car for half an hour or so. Why would I take chances and drive completely exhausted after a hard day at work in construction? It makes no sense.

Another point I'd like to make is about the highway shoulders. According to recent data taken from the AAA Foundation for Traffic Safety, approximately 12 percent of all interstate highway deaths are caused by a vehicle using the shoulder. As it is well-known, it is illegal to drive on a shoulder, unless there's a sign that reads otherwise, and we should not only stay away from shoulder lanes, but also be aware of drivers rushing on them. On that note, I do have a proof that speaks for itself. Look at the video called "Insane Driving on the Shoulder" (https://youtu.be/g5cvw2OMeW4). I was driving in the far right lane of a freeway flooded with heavy traffic, and all of a sudden a white vehicle went past on the shoulder at insane speed. It is transparent that whoever drove this white vehicle didn't care about their own safety or that of the rest of the people on the road. On that day, it was just a matter of luck, and I am thankful that I didn't get into a car accident.

The video called "Speeding on the shoulder" shows a similar situation (https://youtu.be/dYxTzS4oG7k). Unlike the one above, this video displays how ruthless and careless some drivers can be. You can see that even though there was no traffic, a black sedan was still using a shoulder lane, and on top of that, sped faster than other vehicles. Isn't that weird? The next question should be: why would someone drive on a shoulder lane when there was no traffic? The answer is simple: **people don't care**. Again, some drivers take driving for granted, not realizing that their improper speeding may create risky moments for everyone around them. In hindsight: **be aware of drivers who may speed on shoulder lanes or merge onto other lanes with excessive speed, as this can cause additional frustration.**

The next video on this note is "Speeding on the shoulder, again" (https://youtu.be/STArgSKeYw8). This snippet looks pretty identical to the ones above and the reason why I am including it in this book is to show you how reckless drivers could be on a daily basis. This issue has been increasing for the past couple of years, and it looks like no one has a problem with it. While driving on a shoulder lane is just illegal, killing someone on a road is a felony. However, it seems like some drivers don't consider this fact as something important, which can increase the chances of them becoming involved in similar situations. Are we waiting this to happen? I mean, are we waiting for someone to die as a result of reckless speeding on the shoulders? What do you think?

Another story takes me back in 2016 when I was working in the construction field. At that time, I left my vehicle at the office of the company I worked for, and the foreman Jim, drove us to the construction field where we worked. One day, Jim and I hopped into the construction van, and headed to work. Jim took the expressway as usual and I occupied the passenger's seat as it was the only available place someone could sit due to the van being filled with construction materials. As Jim drove, I saw something in the expressway that made me speechless. I observed the vehicle next to us. The driver of this vehicle was a young woman, perhaps in her mid-twenties. She ate soup from a bowl, balanced on her lap, using one hand to grip the steering wheel and eating with the other. I couldn't believe my eyes and asked myself the question, *"Why would you eat soup while driving on a highway? Was it really that important?"* Frankly speaking, I wouldn't believe this story if someone had told it to me. Even though I saw it with my own eyes, I still can't comprehend how such a thing could really happen.

2. Driving in the City

Driving in the city can be challenging and you have to watch out for all the types of drivers that I walked you through in chapter 3. You also have to keep an eye open for pedestrians and cyclists. On that note, pedestrians tend to jaywalk during a red light, and cyclists often ignore traffic lights—it happens all the time. Furthermore, when you are making turns or simply merging from a side street into a large busy street you have to make sure that it is clear and safe for you to proceed. If you don't have clear visibility do not take any action, as cars could be coming from a spot that initially looks safe. Not only this, but you have to constantly maintain a safe distance from others. On this note something important comes to mind: **always maintain a safe distance from the driver ahead of you as the things may become challenging and having enough time and space for a reaction is crucial.** Also, it is essential to let ambulances, firetrucks, and police to go ahead of you with their sirens on. Particularly, when you have a green light, and sirens can be heard nearby, it implies that a law enforcement vehicle or ambulance is approaching and you should give them the right of way. Oftentimes, I have seen vehicles disregarding ambulances' sirens and trying to pass through busy intersections when the ambulances are honking loudly to alert that everyone on the street should wait for them. Another important subject that you may encounter when you drive in the large cities is private tow trucks. These drivers can be so impatient at times, leading them to make unforeseen maneuvers in order to keep going, such as blowing red lights, excessive speeding, and driving on the shoulders.

Speaking of driving in urban areas, something else I have to reiterate: if you are lost in the city and not sure what your GPS is showing, pull over somewhere in a safe location and look closely at which streets you are driving to. Please, don't try to figure out the streets while driving if you are confused because then you are becoming a distracted driver and that would put your life and those of others in danger.

3. Parking Lots

Parking lots can be very dangerous at times. I have witnessed many situations when cocky and impatient drivers tend to rush out from parking lots because they are too anxious to get to their destinations. Perhaps they had a long day at work and rushing out the parking lot of a grocery store is at the top of their agenda. This is why you should pay attention to them when you find yourself at the parking lot of a big store. Again, by "pay attention," I mean throw a quick glimpse; don't stare at other drivers because something may happen while you are watching them.

For instance, you could inadvertently get involved in a car accident with another driver who has just entered the same parking lot. Also, many times impatient drivers may back up their cars without watching or simply having a wrong perception of what is happening around them. This is why I urge you to take only a quick glimpse at them. As we covered this earlier, many impatient drivers disregard the stop signs in parking lots and just drive without stopping. If you happen to see an impatient driver speeding in a parking lot, and there is a stop sign a few feet from them, then they will most likely ignore the sign and continue on their mission, which perhaps is to leave the parking lot as soon as possible. People nowadays are minding their own business and do not care whether they cut you off or just simply put you and themselves in risky situations. This is why, as a safe driver, your purpose is to acknowledge them and keep your distance from such drivers. As you keep practicing these methods it will slowly become natural to you and you will find yourself avoiding unpleasant situations and car accidents more often—this is the beautiful art of being a safe driver.

4. Suburbs

Driving in suburbs also can be challenging at times because people there drive in certain way. What do

I mean by that? Suburbs are like small villages and people from these towns will have unique driving habits. They are accustomed to driving in the same lane, the same speed, and going to the same places. Don't get me wrong, though; I am not criticizing the suburban drivers. In fact, there is nothing wrong with their driving habits—I am simply sharing with you my knowledge to help you became a better driver. That is all.

It is also important to emphasize that suburbs usually don't have much traffic, but when a particular road becomes congested due to construction, then suburban drivers can feel overwhelmed by the additional traffic. They often become mad and impatient because they are used to drive on empty roads. Also, drivers in the burbs typically mind their own business and are often willing to let you go in front of them or allow you to merge from a side street into a large and busy road. However, there may be moments where they don't acknowledge you and refuse to let you go for no apparent reason. As a safe driver, it is important to keep in mind these principles.

5. Driving in Bad Neighborhoods

What actually are bad neighborhoods? These, in my opinion, are areas where the potential for danger is higher. People living there may suffer from mental illness, or face financial struggles, and drivers tend toward aggressive and reckless driving behaviors. Some neighborhoods can be run-down and well-known to be ridden with crime. For this reason, driving in these neighborhoods could be challenging at times. This is something that is not typically covered in driving schools, but it is important to mention that in some areas, people may drive without insurance or even a driver's license. Please note that this is a general statement and is not meant to single out a particular ethnicity or religion.

Driving in a bad neighborhood, you may encounter someone who is driving aggressively in a car that is worth $1,000. This may imply that the person does not care about their car and possibly does not have auto insurance. As a safe driver, you need to acknowledge those types of drivers and just keep in mind that they may not be completely legit. Avoid drivers like this, as you may get involved in a car wreck and find yourself in a hit-and-run situation where the other driver flees the scene, often without auto insurance or even a valid driver's license. Trust me, I know this from firsthand experience.

6. Driving in Rich Neighborhoods

Driving in rich neighborhoods is fun but it also can be challenging. Speeding, for instance, is likely to be seen in wealthy areas, and drivers there can be easily frustrated for whatever reason. Not only this, but something else comes in mind. In those neighborhoods, the police don't have much to do as crime activity is minimal, resulting in troopers lingering around for the most part, I would say. This reminds me of something that happened in 2019. I was driving a passenger to Winnetka, IL. I pulled into a private driveway and parked my vehicle at a large house. It was dark that day, as dusk had fallen, reducing the visibility. Right after I dropped the passenger off, I reversed my vehicle and noticed headlights from another vehicle that was difficult to identify. Even though I couldn't recognize the vehicle, I already had an idea what it might be, and because I was curious, I decided to drive past the mysterious vehicle. As you might already guessed, it was a police officer who immediately did a U-turn after I passed him. Over the next couple of minutes, the cop tailgated me as I drove slowly. In that moment, I was telling myself, "I bet he's checking me out!" The next minute, the cop flashed the police lights and pulled me over. I couldn't help but wonder why the officer would stop me, considering that I had all the necessary stickers and permits in place. The officer walked by and I studied the person. It was a man in his late thirties who stared me with an angry expression on his face as though I just deeply offended him. Then, the man asked me the usual question if I knew why he had stopped me, to which I answered that I had no idea. The trooper explained that the light of my license's plate had burned out and after a few minutes he let me go with a warning. I thanked the man and headed back to the city. That was the first time a cop pulled me over in four years driving in Illinois. But what point am I making here? **In wealthy neighborhoods, it is more likely to be pulled over, even though you are following the road laws.**

7. Alleys

As you may know, alleys are often seen as shortcut options that many drivers tend to use. However, alleys can be very tricky. Here is my piece of advice—avoid alleys. Why? Because construction vans tend to use alleys for whatever reason and they seem to drop screws and other sharp metal objects there. If you go through an alley, I guarantee you will have a flat tire the next day. I can speak from my own experience and declare that I have changed dozens of my vehicle's tires because of these types of roads. Yes, some alleys in downtown Chicago are cleaned regularly and can be considered safe, but most of the alleys around the side streets are not cleaned and that can put you in an unpleasant situation. As I said earlier, stay away from them.

Here is a story I'd like to share with you. One particular day, I was driving for Lyft and I had a ride request a few minutes away. On that day, the traffic was horrible and I decided to go through an alley for a shortcut. As soon as I turned into it, I saw the back of a red Dodge Ram truck that was stopped in the alley, blocking the entire passage. Carefully, I watched what the truck was about to do. In the next second, I was shocked. The truck was backing up and coming at me. I said to myself, "*This person doesn't see me!*" As soon as I realized this, I immediately honked, but the truck didn't seem to hear my warning. And so I put my vehicle in reverse, trying to avoid a potential car accident. I turned my vehicle away as fast as I could. While I was backing up, I wasn't completely safe, and that's when the Ram hit my fender. After the accident, I jumped out of my car to survey the damages. The front bumper and the fender were smashed. The driver who hit me was a young man who had been blasting hip-hop music in his truck and that is why he hadn't heard the honking, which brings me back to the point that honking one's horn isn't always a helpful solution in a situation like this. It turned out that the driver of the Ram was irresponsible, driving a brand new truck with expired insurance, which get to the point that I had to pay for the repairs out of my own pocket. The point I am making here is that I shouldn't have used the alley because it was not safe way to get to my destination.

Another interesting point is that some drivers may come out of an alley without looking or waiting for you. It has happened to me a couple of times already when I was driving on a side street, and all of a sudden a driver darts out of an alley without looking, causing me to hit the brakes. Fortunately, I do have a video that proves my point and shows how drivers just come out from alleys without looking or acknowledging if other drivers are close by. Go to my YouTube channel and play the video called "Coming out from an alley" (https://youtu.be/uzt4mfL4L9k). On my left side, you can see a dark-red colored SUV coming out of the alley and merging onto the side street where I was driving. The SUV driver didn't see me and drove in front of my vehicle, causing me to stop and wait for him. Again, this is the beautiful art of being a safe driver. Acknowledge the driver and wait for him to go. That's the power! This SUV driver wasn't smarter than me just because he drove before me, absolutely not. I am the smarter driver in that situation because I observe the entire situation and smoothly let him go without causing any frustration. This is why it is important to slow down when approaching alleys because you never know if someone will be carelessly emerging in front of you.

Conclusion: alleys may look convenient at first, but in the long run there is a higher chance of having a flat tire, a fender bender or worse.

8. Driving in Crowded Places

Driving in crowded places is challenging and often can be frustrating because the heavy traffic seems like it will never end. As an experienced driver, I suggest you avoid taking your vehicle into crowded areas such as football stadiums, music concerts, large convention centers, etc. In those situations, other drivers get overwhelmed by the traffic, people around you walk between the vehicles, screaming and drinking while you are trying to find a parking spot among the chaos. As I mentioned earlier, you should avoid overcrowded areas. However, if you do happen to find yourself stuck in similar situation, be very careful; try to avoid looking at your phone while driving and keep an eye out for literally everything around you. Just imagine, if an accident occurs while you are stuck in traffic, you could find yourself trapped in a nightmare. Even if it is not your fault, it can take you some time for the street to clear out. Imagine your vehicle broken down in the middle of a crowded area—that perhaps would be your worst nightmare because it would take some time before a tow truck could come and drag your vehicle out of the crowded place.

Here is another interesting story: I remember a day before Christmas in 2017 when I got stuck in heavy traffic somewhere in downtown Chicago. At that time, I used to work for a Greek guy, and he happened to be the driver. On that day, the traffic was something else. I mean, it was epic. It took us an hour and a half to just get out of the crowded downtown. Every single intersection was blocked; green light, red light—it didn't matter. People were yelling at each other because it took forever to move just a couple of feet with their vehicles. Bottom line: the picture didn't look good. Actually, I was glad that I wasn't the driver but simultaneously felt bad for the Greek guy who was trying to find a way out of the chaotic streets. We arrived at the office way too late as expected, but at least nothing bad happened, aside from spending too much time in traffic.

Another situation in my driving experience goes back to 2015 when I was driving home from work. On that day, there was a nasty blizzard and the traffic became horrible—a nightmare. The GPS showed a two-miles distance from my current location to home, but it took much longer as the vehicles were barely moving. Fortunately, nothing really happened, but the thought that I could have had an accident gave me the chills all the way down to my spine. On that day, it took me just about an hour and forty minutes to drive roughly two miles to reach my destination. This actually reminds me to emphasize: **the distance doesn't determine how long a ride would take.**

July in 2022, I had a situation in downtown

Chicago. It was the afternoon on a busy Friday. People were out because the weather was nice, which made the rideshare business in high demand. To make the picture more captivating, I would suggest you go to my YouTube channel and play the video called "Car accident on a busy street" (https://youtu.be/_7qJ4W2WHyo). In this video, I was waiting at a red light in two lanes, each going in a different direction. The driver in front of me, who was in a blue Lexus, didn't analyze the situation well enough and literally stopped in the crosswalk. The Lexus driver acknowledged that and started reversing without noticing that I was behind them. I couldn't go anywhere because another car was right behind me. So, I honked and waved, hoping the Lexus driver would see me. Well, my hopes were useless because the Lexus driver backed into my bumper. In a split second, I jumped out of my car to survey the damages. It wasn't really bad, because the Lexus driver was backing up slowly, but I had to address the situation. So, I walked to the Lexus, wanting to have a word with the driver who had just hit me. The Lexus driver happened to be a young woman who was engrossed in her smartphone when I knocked on her window door to have a word with her. The music in her vehicle was loud, which explained why she didn't hear me when I honked. Nevertheless, the young woman was polite and attentive. We exchanged information and

I headed to the police department to file a report. The cops at the police station were shell-shocked after seeing this video. They couldn't believe that a vehicle would back up at a red light, which is something I have witnessed frequently over the past few years. In hindsight: I should have avoided being in that crowded area, because it caused me to stop working and deal with unnecessary consequences such as filing a police report and speaking with the woman's insurance company. It was an unfortunate experience, but I can't deny that I got lucky, as the damages were not significant—just a scratch.

The video named "Extremely difficult situation" has something crucial that needs to be acknowledged (https://youtu.be/OOv2oYmSbhs). I was waiting at a green light in the downtown area because the intersection in front of me was blocked by two buses and a couple of cars. At this point, I said to myself, "There is no reason for me to proceed even if I have a green light, as I will get stuck in the intersection, which could create a worse situation." So I waited patiently and hoped the intersection would clear out since I had a passengers with me who had already been in my car for about 50 minutes, waiting for me to pass the intersection to drop them off. After the light turned green for the third time, I was ready to proceed straight ahead, but suddenly a silver SUV stopped behind the bus and blocked almost the entire intersection. It became a nail-biting situation. Fortunately, one lane was left open, and the cars next to me started moving. Taking my time, I proceeded on a yellow, going behind the silver SUV. Now, I didn't just cross the street, as this was a very difficult situation, but I wanted to make sure I had a clear visibility of the cars on my left before I continued, as someone might crash into my vehicle without seeing me. In the end, I crossed the intersection safely, as I was certain that every driver had acknowledged my intentions. This is what it is like to be a safe driver: **you are making your maneuvers in a safe way without causing any risk to others around you.** Following this concept, something else needs to be stated: **in driving, there should be no such thing as assumptions; you have to be certain before making any maneuvers.** I can't stress this enough: before making any maneuvers, such as changing lanes, making turns, reversing, and so on, you have to be absolutely sure that it is safe to do it.

There is another story I'd like to share with you. It was around the spring season in 2019 when I had a ride request to pick-up a passenger from O'Hare. The rideshare app showed me that the passenger was located at Terminal 2, which, at that time, could easily get crowded. Approaching the terminal, I witnessed how congested it had become. There were so many cars that it took me some time to get closer to the passenger. Actually, the number of the cars exceeded the number of the passengers at the terminal. The closer I got, the more cars were stalled in front of me. But the ride promised to be lucrative and I didn't want to miss the chance. So, as I was getting closer, in a blink of an eye someone hit me from the back. I was like, "*Really! Just as I was about to pick the passenger and someone hit me!*" Immediately, I exited my vehicle and walked to my rear bumper to investigate the situation. To my surprise, the damage was barely visible. I saw that the driver who stopped at my bumper was willing to do whatever I said, but I didn't take any action. Instead, I waved at him as if to say, "*It's fine. Don't worry about it.*" Then, I picked up the rider and completed the ride assignment.

Conclusion: as I mentioned earlier, you should avoid crowded places where cars are barely moving and if you happen to be stuck in a similar situation— be extremely careful and keep your eyes open.

CHAPTER 7

Driving in Bad Weather Conditions

According to the US Department of Transportation, about 21% of all vehicle crashes are caused by hazardous weather conditions, resulting in an average of over 5,000 deaths and 418,000 injuries annually. That said, I think weather conditions need to be acknowledged and not taken for granted. So, let's break down each one of them.

1. Rain

Heavy downpours can be very dangerous due to reduced visibility. Not only that, but they can also lead to a situation where you may lose control of your vehicle. So what could be a possible reason to lose control of your vehicle as it rains? First and foremost—your tires. If the tread of your tires is worn out, this could cause huge problems as your car may not be able to stop properly. This is why it is important to keep your tires up to date. I remember years ago when I drove my first car, which I had bought in the US. At that time, I was working as an electrician and didn't pay much attention to my vehicle until one particular rainy day. At a four-way stop-sign intersection, my car suddenly slipped, and for a moment, I lost traction. I was completely puzzled. Caught off guard, I quickly jumped out of the vehicle to inspect it and discovered that my tires were in desperate need of replacement. From that moment on, I always make sure that my tires have good tread. As a safe driver, you should always have good tires because things could go sideways, literally.

There is one more thing I need to point out when it comes to bad weather conditions such as rain, and that is the large puddles. You might ask yourself, "Why?" Avoiding puddles is important because there's a higher chance of encountering a large pothole, which can completely damage your tires and suspension.

It's also crucial to adjust your vehicle's heating or air conditioning, whichever suits the moment, in order to prevent steamy windows, which could reduce your visibility. To do this, make sure to press the button that directs the airflow towards your windows, not just inside your car.

It goes without saying that driving in the rain with worn-out windshield wipers can turn into a nightmare because you wouldn't be able to see anything. So, if you go somewhere in a long trip or simply heading to the closest supermarket, it is vital to have your worn out wiper blades replaced. Otherwise, it could be really annoying.

Another important thing to keep in mind is that if your car has been parked outdoors for a few hours during a rainy day, you should pump the brakes a couple of times before hitting the road. This may seem unnecessary, but it's actually a safety measure. The reason for this is that the brake pads could be filled with water, which can affect your car's braking performance. By pumping the brakes, you're helping to get rid of any excess water in the brake pads, which can prevent a potential safety hazard while driving. So, make sure to pump the brakes a few times before starting your journey to ensure your brakes are working effectively.

Of course, flooded roads should be avoided, especially if you drive a sedan. I remember years ago my hometown got flooded because it had been raining for a while and the sewer system wasn't the greatest, which made the entire city feel like Venice. At that time, I must have been around 10 years old, sitting in the back seat of our family vehicle, which was also the cab that Dad made a living from. My father was driving back to our apartment, and when we were around 200 feet away, the car stuck on a flooded street. It was a horrible moment because when we opened the vehicle's doors to survey what was happening, the car started to fill with water. The water level must have been more than two feet high, but it was just enough to freak my mother out. Concerned, Dad had to send my mom and me home while he had to stay in his cab, waiting for a tow truck because the engine had taken in too much water. It was a wild time for all of us. However, I am thankful that we didn't have to swim to our apartment.

Conclusion: driving in the rain can be difficult at times. Do not underrate wet or flooded areas, as you can find yourself stuck somewhere and then you have to wait hours for a tow truck.

2. Hail

Hail can pose a serious threat to both people and vehicles. The irregular lumps of ice falling at incredible speed can cause significant damage to your vehicle and even injure or kill a human being. Moreover, hail can significantly reduce visibility, making driving difficult and risky. Perhaps the next logical question is: what should you do if you are driving when it's hailing? Your best choice is to shelter somewhere, whether under the roof of a gas-station or some type of garage, until it stops hailing. Usually, hailstorms don't last long, just a couple of minutes. So you don't have to hide somewhere for too long. Another question arises: when does it hail? Hailstorms usually occur during the spring season, and they tend to happen during the day. If you notice the sky turning black, as though an apocalypse is coming, it is highly possible that hailstorm is on the way.

3. Fog

The foggy weather should definitely be taken seriously, as your visibility is reduced to a dangerous point where you may found yourself in a very bad situation. It is important to keep the speed limit when it is fogging and turn on your low-beam headlights so other drivers can see you better. Important note: **avoid driving with high-beam lights while driving in foggy conditions as they may reduce your visibility**.

Keeping a long distance from other cars is also a good practice when it comes to driving in fog, as it may be necessary to make sudden stops due to changes in traffic ahead. In cases of severely dense fog, where the visibility is significantly reduced and the weather conditions have progressively deteriorated, making it difficult for you to proceed, it is better to pull over into a safe area, such as a gas station, and wait for the fog to clear. However, if you end up driving in a foggy weather, be on high alert as the things can get messy, especially in outback areas where you may come across a deer or other animal crossing your way.

4. Snow

According to the National Highway Traffic Safety Administration (NHTSA), around 17% of all vehicle crashes occur during winter weather conditions such as snow, sleet, and ice. These accidents can result in serious injuries and fatalities.

In the United States, the Federal Highway Administration (FHWA) estimates that there are over 116,000 injuries and 1,300 fatalities each year due to car accidents that occur during snowy or icy weather conditions.

As you can see, snow is certainly one of the most challenging weather conditions you could face while driving. Just like rain, driving in snow requires good tires. If your tires are not good enough, it's better to avoid traveling during snowfall because your vehicle may not be able to stop properly. This applies to SUVs as well. I have been witnessing that many people drive when it snows as though it is dry, sunny weather, which perhaps was why some of them end up getting into a car accident. As a safe driver, it is important to avoid speeding in snow, as your vehicle may easily slide sideways on the road. Abrupt braking should also be avoided as it can cause you to lose control of your vehicle, especially if you are driving at 40 miles per hour or faster. Also, when taking a steep ramp exit off of a snow-covered highway, it is best to avoid frequent braking and unnecessary speeding. Instead, let your vehicle go smoothly, or you might be surprised as your car loses traction. It is best to maintain a safe distance from vehicles ahead of you because other drivers may slide dangerously, and by keeping distance from them, you will have time to react and avoid getting hit if needed it. It is important to be able to slow your vehicle down if it becomes necessary. Reducing speed on snowy roads is crucial as it can save you a lot of frustration, but it has to be done smoothly. As I mentioned earlier, hitting the brakes abruptly can cause your vehicle to lose traction. Depending on how bad the weather is and if the streets are covered with snow, you have to apply the brakes gently. A lot of car accidents happen during blizzards when drivers fail to stop their vehicles properly. This is a serious topic, and people should practice slowing their vehicle down responsibly.

As I write this, the vehicle I am currently driving has a semi-automatic transmission, which allows me to reduce and increase speed manually. Even though I am comfortable with driving on snowy roads, I avoid going anywhere in snow unless it is an emergency. Why? Because I am aware that other drivers can be indifferent about weather conditions and may drive recklessly or cut me off, which could put me in an unpleasant situation.

Conclusion: driving on snowy streets could be

dangerous, and I recommend you avoid driving in heavy snow unless it's an emergency.

5. Sleet and Ice

As you may already know, sleet is something between rain and snow, but it can be more dangerous because it is hard to recognize at times. Sleet on the road looks like it has been raining for a while and people oftentimes get confused. In these types of weather conditions, your vehicle can easily lose traction, especially if you are speeding. Obviously, the next question is: how do you recognize a street covered in sleet? Walk outside on the street and try to slide a bit by using your own legs as though you are skating, and if you feel like you are on an ice skating rink, then you know that you are dealing with a sleet-covered road. But don't overdo it! I don't want you to fall and break something because of my advice. This is just for a small test, and even if you only take a few steps on a sleet covered terrain, you will be able to tell if it is sleet or just rain. In hindsight: the most essential part that you should know about sleet is to avoid unnecessary speeding while driving.

Now let's talk about ice. Unlike sleet, ice can be easily recognized. Icy roads are just as dangerous as sleet-covered ones, but there is a slight difference. Driving on an icy road, you have to be very careful and don't push the gas too abruptly as it could cause your vehicle to lose traction. Remember: be extremely cautious when you find yourself driving on icy roads and avoid hitting the brakes abruptly as you may lose control of your vehicle. Something else needs to be pointed out here: **don't just rely on good tires when it comes to driving on icy roads.**

6. Tornados

According to Stormaware.mo.gov, tornadoes cause an average of 70 fatalities and 1,500 injuries in the U.S. each year. The strongest tornadoes have rotating winds of more than 250 mph. They can be more than one mile wide and stay on the ground for over 50 miles. Before a tornado hits, the wind may die down and the air may become very still. A cloud of debris can mark the location of a tornado even if a funnel is not visible. Tornadoes generally occur near the trailing edge of a thunderstorm. It is not uncommon to see clear, sunlit skies behind a tornado. Now, the most logical question here is: what you should do when a tornado is approaching while you are in your vehicle? First and foremost, you should immediately take action and leave your vehicle. Hiding in your car is definitely not a good option, as it may potentially rolls over at a high speed. Run and seek a shelter such as a tunnel under a highway or an overpass, but stay away from gas stations, as they can be brutally destroyed or damaged by the approaching tornado.

Also, make sure you have your phone with you as you can use it to track the meteorology updates. Following these steps should help you stay safe during a destructive tornado. However, I sincerely hope that you will never have to experience any of them for the rest of your life.

CHAPTER 8

Important Tips about Keeping Your Vehicle Well-Maintained

In this chapter I will walk you through important pieces of advice to which you should pay attention while you are on the road. First things first, let's talk about mechanical issues that may occur while you are driving.

1. Grinding Noises

When you hear noises that sound like something is grinding, in most cases that means your brake pads needs to be changed. So, depending on from which end the noises come, it could be the front or the rear brakes. Of course, it can be something else as well, so it is vital to check your vehicle with your local auto shop. In my opinion, every time I hear grinding noises it turns out to be the brake pads. The next question comes to mind: how often should you change your brake pads? Usually, the brake pads should be changed between 45,000 and 50,000 miles. I change them every 90,000 miles because I buy brake pads directly from the dealer, which means the quality is the best on the market and they have extended endurance. Important note: **if you hear the grinding noises, you should immediately change the brake pads because if you don't, your brake calipers may damage the disks, and that can cost you more money for a repair.**

2. Clunking

Clunking noises could came from many components of your vehicle. One source of the noise could be the sway bar links. You should immediately contact your auto shop and notify them about this issue because it can become progressively worse. If you only hear a clunking noise when the vehicle is turning, that can be the CV Axle, which also needs to be replaced as soon as possible.

3. Battery

Obviously, if you drive a Tesla or any other electric vehicle you don't need to read this. However, if you drive a gasoline vehicle and leave any lights on, then the following morning you would find yourself struggling to fire up the engine because the battery is now dead. You can always check your battery at

AutoZone, O'Railys and any other auto store. To my recollection, it is still free as I am writing this.

4. The Alternator

If your vehicle shuts off while you are driving the problem most likely is from the alternator because it doesn't generate enough electric power, which your car needs to run. The first car I bought in the U.S. gave me the same problem. It was shutting down intermittently while I was driving. It was a nightmare. Just image how awful could be if the engine of your vehicle is not working while you are on the road. It could drive you nuts. Replacing the alternator should be the solution. However, you should always consult with your auto shop.

5. Loud Noises

When you hear loud noises coming from your vehicle as though it is like a racing car, then it most likely the problem is the muffler. Several times, I had this issue on my previous cars, and after repairing the muffler the annoying loud noise was gone. That being noted, it is typical for old cars with high mileage to require work on the muffler.

6. Alignment

Alignment is an important maintenance task that needs to be performed on vehicles to ensure their safe and efficient operation. The alignment of a vehicle's wheels refers to the adjustment of the angles of the tires relative to the vehicle's chassis and each other. It usually needs to be done once in a year or depending on how much you drive. If your vehicle becomes a little unstable on the road and you feel it is difficult to keep it on one lane or if it feels like your vehicle is moving slightly on one side when you driving straight, then your wheels need alignment. You can definitely tell the difference once your vehicle has completed an alignment. It feels smooth and easy to control.

7. Cracking.

Cracking noises can come from various components. However, as a general rule of thumb, it is possible that the noise is coming from the belt tensioner. What is this actually? The belt tensioner is an essential component of a vehicle's engine accessory drive system. Its primary function is to maintain the proper tension of the engine's accessory drive belts, which transfer power from the engine's crankshaft to the alternator, power steering pump, air conditioning compressor, and other components.

After you hear cracking noises you should immediately pull your vehicle over, open the hood, and examine the belt-tensioner which usually is located above the alternator. Although your vehicle may still be drivable, it is important to call for roadside assistance if you hear cracking noises from the belt-tensioner. Continuing to drive could cause your vehicle to break down after just a few blocks. In this case, it is essential to replace the belt tensioner and the auxiliary belt that goes with it to avoid any further issues with your vehicle.

8. Engine Oil

Unless you drive an electric car, engine oil and oil filter should be replaced every 4,000 to 5,000 miles. This method is important as you keep the life of the engine longer and avoid any further problems. Full synthetic is required, especially if you drive a new vehicle. However, you should always discuss what type of oil you need with your auto mechanic. Important note: **if you drive a lot of miles on a daily basis, especially during summertime, your vehicle can burn oil, which means that it needs more, but not much.** Allow me to ask you this question: have you ever seen a nasty cloud of smoke coming out from a car's muffler? Have you ever wonder why smoke can billowed out of car's muffler? Here is the answer. For the most part, gray smoke coming out of the muffler of your vehicle means that your engine is burning oil. If the smoke is black, then your car is burning gasoline. I would suggest you contact your auto mechanic if you see any smoke coming from the muffler of your vehicle. On this note, you should regularly check the level of the motor oil to make sure it hasn't been burned; otherwise, your engine will break, causing an expensive repair.

9. Overheating

Allow me to ask you this: have you seen a vehicle in flames? If you have, then you know how scary a burning car can be. Usually, the reason why is because a vehicle has been overheated. That is a serious problem, and if you do not know what to do in similar situations, then you may end up in a car being on fire. With these thoughts in mind, let me share a story. It was the summertime in 2022. As I was driving to pick up a passenger, I looked at the dashboard and what I saw got me concerned. The little arrow in the temperature gauge was moving close to "H," which, as you know, stands for hot. I then realized that my vehicle was being overheated. So what did I do? I simply canceled the ride request, pulled into a safe place and turned the engine off. I waited for my car to cool off. After thirty minutes of waiting, I started my vehicle and immediately headed to my mechanic. Unfortunately, I couldn't go far as my vehicle overheated again which caused me to pull over and turn off the engine for the second time. I waited for the engine to cool down and drove to my guy. I had to repeat this process for several times until I got to the mechanic. After a quick examination of my vehicle, the mechanic told me that the thermostat, which has the function of maintaining a suitable temperature in the car's engine, broke down and needed to be replaced. At that time, I paid $60 for a new thermostat and $40 for labor, making the total cost of the repair $100. After that, my car was back on the road. On that day, if I hadn't turned off the engine of my vehicle to cool down and just kept driving, then surely my car would have been in flames.

Conclusion: watch the temperature gauge in your vehicle's dashboard and if the arrow points to "H" pull over as soon as possible and turn off the engine. In that case, I would suggest calling for a roadside assistance, unless you are very close to your auto shop and willing to take the risk of driving with several stops like I did.

10. Other Components

Here are some of your car's components that need routine checking. One of them is the headlights and the taillights or as they call them "brake lights." It's essential to ensure that all of your lights are working as you may be pulled over by a law-enforcement official. Also, keep an eye on the antifreeze level and refill if it is too low. Without antifreeze, your vehicle may not start during cold weather. Another important note: **make sure you do not mix the antifreeze with**

windshield fluid because this can lead to serious damages in your vehicle. For example—pouring windshield fluid instead of antifreeze can harm the cooling system, requiring replacement of many components linked to that system. Trust me, I know this from firsthand experience.

CHAPTER 9

Mastering Your Skills

So what do I mean by mastering your skills? This is a term that refers of how far you have come on the journey of turning into a safe driver. After you read all the chapters and applied all of the techniques, now you get the idea of what it is to be a safe driver. You have learned how to watch for all the types of drivers around you and how to avoid them. You maintain composure and you feel absolutely comfortable behind the steering wheel. Not only this but you also start paying more attention to what is happening around you and became self-aware of each detail on the road. You constantly check your side mirrors and the rearview mirror, and you also ensure clear visibility before performing any type of maneuvers. Furthermore, you excel among other drivers because you know what to do in difficult and challenging situations. And now it is time to master your skills and qualities as a safe driver. On this note, something essential comes to mind: **the more you drive the better driver you will become.** In this chapter, I'll take you through the skills that you need to master yourself.

One of the important aspects of mastering your skills is controlling the traffic around you. What does that even mean? Controlling the traffic is simply letting other drivers go when the situation is difficult in order to improve and clear the traffic in front of you. Let me show you an example to make the things more transparent. Go to my YouTube channel and look at the video called "Controlling the traffic" (https://youtu.be/t9EzIaM2sz4). You can see how I let the gray truck on my right side go and immediately after that I let a black Range Rover make a left turn because it was about to block the one lane street from the ongoing direction. After you have watched this short video, please rewind it and observe how smoothly I handled the entire situation. It didn't take much time for me to wait, I also didn't end up being late. Instead, thanks to my actions, I cleared the traffic in both directions and made the situation easy and smooth, as if I were living in a utopian world where everything is nice and beautiful. This is how you master your skills. You become fully aware of what is happening around you, and you know what to do, making it easier for everybody. What can I say? It is a win-win situation.

Another video called "Let someone go on Mannheim Road" shows an interesting situation.

(https://youtu.be/1NEd17RVnNM). In the video, I was driving in the far right lane on a busy street. On my left side, I noticed that the cars were waiting and it immediately crossed my mind that another vehicle might be waiting to make a left turn. In fact, I was absolutely sure that there must be a car there so I approached slowly, and sure enough, I was right. A red SUV was waiting to make a left turn. I let the red SUV make the turn and not only did I help this driver, but I also helped myself by avoiding an unpleasant situation where a car accident may occur. This is the art of being a safe driver—you are self-aware, knowing what is about to happen and handle the situation smoothly—no muss no fuss. Isn't that beautiful? Now, I have to emphasize something crucial: the red SUV driver, whom I referred earlier, was handling the situation properly as well. This driver didn't just make the left turn, as they were AWARE that someone might be approaching. This brings up the point that the red SUV driver didn't have clear visibility, and therefore hadn't made the left turn immediately. Instead, they waited to see if someone would let them go, in this case, me.

Let's look at another example. Go to my YouTube channel and play the video called "Let someone go, easy" (https://youtu.be/5HnDibVizPg). In the video, you can see how I let someone go by flashing my headlights. The driver in front of me flashed their headlights back as a "thank you" note and made their left turn. This is what I call "street communicating" which means that you are communicating with others while you are on a particular street. I would suggest to rewind this video and play it again. The reason why I am asking you to do this is because I want you to comprehend how smoothly I handle the entire situation without even hitting the brakes. I will reiterate: this is the beauty of being a safe driver.

The video called "Let someone go from a side street" shows an interesting situation (https://youtu.be/ng2NJzcszcU). As I slowly drove, I noticed a red vehicle which was standing on my left side. The red vehicle was coming from a side street and waited to make a left turn. Seeing that there were no cars coming from the oncoming direction, I waved at the red vehicle, signaling for them to go ahead of me. As you can see, I handled the situation smoothly, but there is something important that I need to emphasize: **I wouldn't wave at the red vehicle to go if there were cars coming from the other lane.** This is because it might confuse the red vehicle's driver and potentially cause an accident. If there were other cars present, then I would simply leave enough space for the red vehicle to go and let them figure out on their own when it is safe to make the left turn. This may seem unimportant at first, but it does make a difference when it comes to letting other drivers know what the situation is. Of course, the other driver should always figure their way out, but it is essential to not confuse them and avoid any potential accidents.

Now, let's look at another example. Play the video named "Let someone go from across the street" (https://youtu.be/XKtFPzrEADk). In this snippet, you can see how I drive on a two-lane street with traffic flowing in each direction. As I was driving, I slowed down my vehicle because I have noticed that the vehicles in the other lane had stopped. In my mind, I have already determined that a vehicle might be waiting from a side street to make a left turn. Indeed, as it shows in the video, a black SUV driver was waiting to make a left turn. Technically, I couldn't see that vehicle coming. You can replay the video: there was no sign of the black SUV coming from the side street. Then, how did I know that? Again, this is the power of being a safe driver. You basically know what to do in similar situations where a vehicle may be waiting to make a left turn, so simply you just slow down a little—not to a complete stop because that may piss off the driver behind you.

Up to this point, we have covered situations on which you should let another vehicle go, but what about giving space to large vehicles such as buses or semi-trucks? Please, do me a favor and watch the video dubbed "BUS making a hard right turn" (https://youtu.be/1T1Ks2JccVg). In the video, I was waiting to make a left turn on a red light. On the left side, a long bus was trying to do a hard right turn. In this scenario, I had to reverse my vehicle and give enough space for the bus to make the right turn since it was a tight intersection. As you can tell, I did the maneuver easily since there was no one behind me, and the bus completed its turn. Piece of cake, right? But what would I have done if there was a vehicle behind me? Then, I would simply wave at the driver, waiting behind me, to move their vehicle so that we could both leave enough space for the bus to make the maneuver. Another point needs to be emphasized here: when you find yourself waiting in the left lane and notice a big commercial truck with a large trailer attempting to make a sharp right turn from your left, it is crucial to provide them with enough space so they will be able to complete their right turn maneuver. If you notice that the truck needs more space to successfully complete the turn, you can reverse your vehicle, but only if you there is enough distance from the vehicle behind you. You have to be careful in these situations, as many times, the distance between the truck making the right turn and your vehicle is just a couple of inches. In every case, we should all let a large vehicle make the right turn, as we can't let it block the entire intersection.

Extremely Difficult Situations

Now let's discuss some rare situations that can be much more difficult. In some cases, you may find yourself in an extremely difficult situation, such as making a left from one intersection to another with very little space between them. In moments like this, you have to think quickly and keep moving to clear your vehicle from the intersection. To make it more captivating, I uploaded a video on my YouTube channel called "Extremely dangerous situation" (https://youtu.be/d0fFaWUI7Pg). As you can see, I was already waiting to make a left turn at a busy intersection. You may be asking: what is so special about this video? Hear me out. From the opposite direction, I saw a red vehicle making a right turn and stopped just in a few feet away because there was another intersection with a red light at that moment. Now, I found myself in a really difficult situation because even if I made the left turn, I didn't have enough space, as the red vehicle had already made the right turn, and occupied all the space I needed. So, I patiently waited for the cars coming from the opposite direction, making sure I had clear visibility, and then I made the left turn, leaving my vehicle behind the red car. The light already turned red, but now I was in a nail-biting situation because my car was in the intersection, partially blocking one of the lanes there. What now? Well, I honked to the red vehicle to acknowledge me so they would move a little further and give me enough space to clear my vehicle from the intersection. Fortunately, the red vehicle's driver noticed me and moved their vehicle to the empty left lane, giving me enough space to sneak in my car and clear out from the intersection where I had previously made the left turn. That was definitely a helluva situation that I managed to handle smoothly. However, as you can see, I wouldn't have been able to do it if the red vehicle's driver didn't contribute, which brings me back to the point: **we all share the roads and our duty is to help each other so everyone would go home safely.**

Speeding Slowly

You may be asking yourself, "What is this guy talking about?" Before I answer the question let me ask you this: have you noticed how cab drivers seem to drive slowly at times, but they somehow are always ahead of you? Well, most likely they were speeding slowly. The term "Speeding slowly" is an old cab drivers' phrase that I learned from my father, the man who knows more facts about cars than I know about myself. It basically means to drive safely and at the same time to move fast by catching green lights or just cruising faster by using the fastest lane on a highway without exceeding the speed limit. Speeding slowly comes after you have developed all the skills you need to be a safe driver. In other words, speeding slowly is when a safe driver hits the gas. But acquiring this skill doesn't happen overnight; it takes time to get there. Perhaps the next logical question should be: how long does it take to develop this skill? The answer is subjective. It depends on how fast you pick up the material. Now, speaking of speeding, something important comes to mind: **speeding increases the chance of getting into a car accident.** No matter how safe driver you are, speeding your vehicle can take you on a roller coaster. For that reason, I wouldn't recommend that you just hop in your vehicle and practice speeding slowly. Let it come to you naturally, like when you fall in love with someone—you don't know how, you just know you love the person. As I mentioned earlier, before practicing speeding slowly you need to become a safe driver.

To better understand "speeding slowly" I'd like to share a story with you. I was on a highway, one day, driving inbound to the city of Chicago. I was with a passenger that day and the traffic was moderate. Then, something caught up my attention, I saw a green Lamborghini that was driving on a highway ahead of me. I also had a chance to glimpse at the person who drove the green Lamborghini—it was a man in his late forties. Anyway. So, I would guess that this man drove the luxury vehicle aggressively to reach his destination faster. But there was one problem—the man was driving on the slowest lane, which didn't help him much. A few minutes later, I passed the luxury vehicle, not because I was driving faster, which technically is impossible with my car, but because I used the fastest lane that got me moving faster. A couple of minutes later, I took an exit ramp and headed to the downtown area. I saw that the green Lambo was taking the same ramp, but it was way too far behind me. It amused me because I didn't even speed my vehicle. This story is a good example of how you can move faster, without even trying. It is the power to use the knowledge of speeding slowly, which reminds me to mention something really important: **speeding slowly isn't about racing with other vehicles or even trying to get somewhere faster, it's the beautiful art of knowing when exactly you need to hit the gas and when to hit the brakes without causing any frustration.**

CHAPTER 10

Repetition Is the Mother of Skill

Repetition is the mother of skill. This phrase speaks for itself. It is important to comprehend that becoming a safe driver won't happen overnight. As I said it before; it takes time, but once you have it and keep practicing what you have learned, it stays with you, it becomes part of you. Again, the keyword here is "repetition." For that reason, I'd suggest you to read this book about 10–15 times, not only to know this material, but also to own it. Studies show that the human brain retains around 7% of what is read, and highlighting the essential concepts mentioned in this book is crucial. Let's break down once more which are the important features any safe driver should gain in their driving portfolio. First and foremost, you need to be comfortable in your vehicle. Then, you have to look at the side mirrors and the rearview mirror, checking the blind zones. Then, before doing anything else, you need to have a clear viability around you. After that while driving on the roads you need to acknowledge and recognize all types of drivers that we covered in chapter 3, especially impatient, cocky, distracted, and inexperienced drivers. Most of them will cut you off and merge to your lane in a risky way, but as long as you notice them it is going to be much easier for you to avoid them. Even when someone cuts you off or does something stupid, you need to learn to accept it without any frustration. Safe drivers control their frustrations and not overreact when they operate their vehicles. Taking deep breaths is the solution of self-control while driving and avoid allowing negative emotions to escalate due to the mistakes or actions of impatient drivers on the road. Also, safe drivers are absolutely aware of what is happening around them as they watch for other drivers, cyclists, pedestrians, animals, and so on. Another point that needs to be emphasized here is that safe drivers always keep a safe distance from others. They understand that something can happen at any second, and having enough space will help them react properly. One more thing, safe drivers are prudent when it comes to driving in bad weather conditions and know what they have to do to assure a safe and comfortable ride. Remember—**the more aware you are, the safer driver you will become.**

What You Should Do after Getting into a Car Accident

This book is designed to help you learn how to avoid getting hit, but what if someone hits you anyway? First and foremost, you should check yourself and the other passengers in your vehicle, as well as the people who were in the vehicle that collided with yours. If someone requires urgent medical attention, call 911 and explain the situation. Now, if there is no need to seek first medical responders, you should communicate with the other driver and exchange all the relevant information such as vehicle details and phone numbers. It is crucial to take pictures of the damages to your vehicle as well as the other vehicle involved in the car wreck. After that, you should call 911 to report the accident and follow the instructions given by the dispatcher. If it is a fender bender and both vehicles are drivable, the 911 dispatch may tell you to go to the nearest police station to file a report. After you have filled out the police report and if you believe the other driver is responsible for the car accident, you should contact their insurance company and file a claim. Once the claim is submitted, the insurance company will assign an insurance adjuster who will contact you to discuss any questions related to your claim. Depending on the insurance company's procedures, you may need to get an appraisal to assess the extent of the damages to your vehicle and the associated costs. Here comes an important breakpoint: if the insurance company instructs you to use their app to submit an estimate, then you have to make sure that what is said on the paperwork aligns with your situation. The tricky thing here is that apps designed by insurance companies are purposely aimed at minimizing the cost of repairing your vehicle. In hindsight: always double-check the information provided by the insurance company, as they may try to manipulate the situation by making changes that aren't favorable to you.

With these thoughts in mind, here comes the crucial point: when the insurance company has to pay you money in your favor, the adjuster always seems to be out of the office or otherwise impossible to reach. And they never call you back. Well, that's not coincidence. In fact, I believe some insurance companies instruct their adjusters to be elusive on purpose. Fortunately, I know a knack that always works to find your adjuster when they don't answer their phone: call the direct line to your insurance company and tell them that you cannot get hold of your adjuster and politely ask if they could send the adjuster a note to call you back. It always works. That said, let me mention something important: when my vehicle was stolen with all of my belongings inside, the adjuster told me that the reimbursement limit for my personal items was $200. That was complete

BS, as I had read the entire policy and sent them a screenshot where it said that the insurance would pay $1000 for the belongings of the insured cardholder. There is more! A month after my vehicle was stolen and deemed a total loss, the insurance company charged me another payment for my auto insurance policy. Isn't that ridiculous? I mean, I don't even have a car anymore and these diabolical people kept on debiting my credit card. Do you see where I am going with this? I am warning you because I want you to be aware that insurance firms are always cunning and will do anything to acquire your money.

The Last Ride

At the moment I am writing this, we are living in a digital era where life feels like science fiction. Today electric cars are much more common on roads, compared with how things were in 2017. Technology is continuously growing, and who can predict what we will be driving in 2040? Flying cars are expected to be for sale by 2030. As you know, jet packs have been already tested in the military, and in England they are being used for medical first responders' assistance in rural areas where a helicopter landing is impossible. However, I firmly believe that we will still be driving cars for the next fifteen years, and possibly even longer. That means we need to learn how to be safe on the road, otherwise someone may get seriously hurt. Again, this is the main reason why I decided to write this book. I hope my guidance will help you overcome a lot of accumulated frustration on the road and bring you home safely. One more thing I'd like to reiterate: **be aware of your surroundings on the road and study the behavior of other drivers. Failing to do so can put your life and the lives of others in danger.**

Author's Note

Some useful information:

**According to NHTSA, 42,939 lives were lost
on U.S. roads in 2021.
Drunk-driving fatalities: 13,384.
Speeding-related: 12,330.**

I hope this book gave you useful information and helps you become a safe driver. If you find this material informative and helpful, please share this book with a friend, as we all need to stay safe on the road and continue living our lives the best we can. Remember: **you are the winner on the roads and that's the end of this book.**

Feel free to subscribe to my YouTube channel to access more videos and intriguing topics about driving in bizarre situations. You can also comment on my videos and share with me what you think. I also would appreciate it if you could leave an honest review on Amazon or Goodreads, as it helps me to develop my future endeavors. Your opinion matters.

Happy driving.

Check Out Dimitry's Other Bestsellers

On Amazon and Everywhere Books Are Sold.

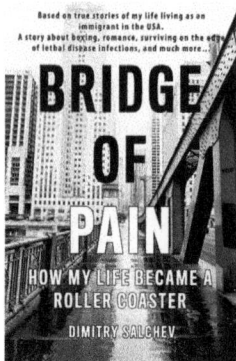

Based on true stories of my life living as an immigrant in the USA. A story about boxing, romance, surviving on the edge of lethal disease infections, and much more...

BRIDGE OF PAIN

HOW MY LIFE BECAME A ROLLER COASTER

DIMITRY SALCHEV

Bridge of Pain: How My Life Became a Roller Coaster

Dimitry's autobiography is based on ten years of his life, and it's primarily focused on the years between 2014 and 2019. Dimitry talks about how he prevailed over countless obstacles in those years. You will witness how his routine life turned into a nightmare. In this book, he portrays how many times he nearly died, and how he returned to life. He also emphasizes how wrong he had been and how important his faith in God was.

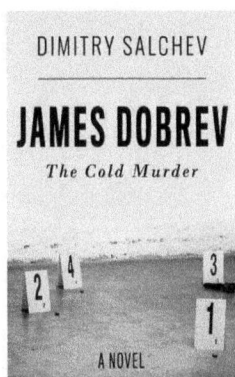

DIMITRY SALCHEV

JAMES DOBREV
The Cold Murder

A NOVEL

James Dobrev: The Cold Murder

James Dobrev was a prosperous author. He lived all of his life in Chicago. One night, he stopped working on his novel for a trip to the closest liquor store. When he got to the store something unpleasant happened. Since then, James' life became a nightmare. He was accidently involved in a murder. The target was a Russian man who had been kidnapped from Moscow. The police detectives couldn't understand how the Russian man looked the same as he had sixty years earlier. The police sent James to Bulgaria for witness protection. His trip to Bulgaria was bizarre. James realized that some people were watching him. Just as things seemed to be going okay, James received shocking news. His mother had disappeared. He had to fly back to Chicago. A few weeks later, one of the most brutal firefights in the history of Illinois occurred.

Dimitry Salchev

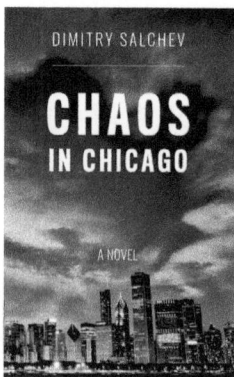

Chaos In Chicago

On the Fourth of July, a young woman is reported missing. Her family has no idea where she might have gone. The police can find no evidence of where she can be. Robert McCarthur and Lisa Fernandez are the detectives assigned to work on finding the missing woman. Along the way in searching for her, more surprises shock them. Many questions arise which seem impossible to answer. Just when it seems things have become too complicated, something crucial happens that no one can explain. This and much more increases the chaos in Chicago.

About the Author

Dimitry Salchev was born and raised in Plovdiv, Bulgaria. He immigrated to the US in 2014. In 2018, he was diagnosed with endocarditis. He was urged to have complicated surgery and had to fight for his life. He had four surgeries in two years. Twice, he had to relearn how to walk. Before his last surgery, he became a hundred percent paralyzed. He lost the ability to talk, see, and move any of his muscles. The doctors thought they were losing him. Nevertheless, Dimitry woke up after two weeks of induced coma. It took him some time to heal after his last surgery. In 2020 he met a beautiful girl. They decided to get married in 2021. Three months after the wedding, his marriage turned into a nightmare. The following year, he tried to work on his marriage with hope that it would be fine. His situation got worse, and he had to move out of his wife's apartment. He had nowhere to go. He was forced to live in his car somewhere in the Chicago area. However, that didn't discourage him. When he came to the US, the author could barely say a word in English, but in 2022, he wrote two books in the same year. During that time, he never quit his job.

In 2023, the author had published two more books, and in the meantime, he was diagnosed with a severe health problem for which he had to undergo surgery to survive. Regardless of what happens to him, Dimitry would not stop writing books. God bless America.

Milton Keynes UK
Ingram Content Group UK Ltd.
UKHW010851211223
434780UK00004B/211

9 798989 115501